FROM SELLING TO MANAGING

FROM SELLING TO MANAGING

REVISED EDITION

Guidelines for the First-Time Sales Manager

Ronald Brown

amacom

American Management Association

This publication is designed to provide accurate and authoritative information in regard to the subject matter covered. It is sold with the understanding that the publisher is not engaged in rendering legal, accounting, or other professional service. If legal advice or other expert assistance is required, the services of a competent professional person should be sought.

Library of Congress Cataloging-in-Publication Data

Brown, Ronald, 1900–
    From selling to managing : guidelines for the first-time sales
manager / Ronald Brown. — Rev. ed.
        p.   cm.
    Includes index.
    ISBN 0-8144-7380-6
    1. Sales Management.   2. Sales personnel.   I. Title.
    HF5438.B825   1990   90-55201
    658.8'1—dc20   CIP

Printing number

10

Contents

(P. Le X dd)

Preface to the Revised Edition

Many sales managers come to their jobs from the ranks of the sales force. They are promoted on the strength of their outstanding performances as salespeople. Few receive formal training for their new responsibilities. They are expected, rather, to make the transition from selling to managing on their own steam.

That's why I wrote this book—to help the newly appointed field sales manager master the job. I concentrate here on the problems managers face and point out what they must do to solve them. It is my hope that the general approaches suggested will stimulate readers to think of ways of adapting them to meet individual requirements.

Since the first edition of *From Selling to Managing* was published, a number of important changes have occurred in the way the world does business:

1. In 1968 there were few women in sales. Today, in many organizations, up to 20 or 30 percent of the sales force are women and between 10 and 15 percent of their sales managers are women. This book has been revised to reflect these new demographics.
2. The desktop computer, the portable computer, the word processor, the fax machine—all these tools were unknown to the field sales manager of 1968. Today they are important

tools of communication and control. How they can be used in many situations to make the work of the sales manager more effective is a recurrent theme of this edition.

3. In many organizations the distributor has become an important cog in the machinery linking sales, distribution, and service. Chapter 2 shows how field sales managers can use their relationship with the distributor to their company's advantage.

The top-notch salesperson has always enjoyed a close relationship with the customer: The customer relies on the sales rep for advice, for solutions to serious problems, and for suggestions on ways of improving operations. Yet in the past, sales reps were trained in little more than knowing their company's "line," writing up orders and reports, and following instructions.

The ongoing technological revolution is changing the way many companies interpret the sales function. It is a lot more technically oriented today. Sometimes this means that it is easier to turn an engineer into a sales rep than to try to teach engineering knowledge to a salesperson. In any case, today's salesperson not only sells, but educates, services, acts as a problem solver, helps the purchaser improve production or distribution, and earns the respect of the buyer through the know-how he or she is capable of displaying. This, of course, if often called Consultative Selling™, as developed by Mack Hanan.

Field sales managers and salespeople work closely together today as planners and communicators, bringing to their collaboration new ideas, solutions to problems, and improvement in procedures and policies. The field sales manager is the arm of the company, the salesperson the finger that touches the buyer far from the main office. To the buyer the sales rep is often "the company." Together, as partners, the sales manager and sales rep strive constantly to improve performance in reaching the objectives they have accepted. It is the job of the field sales manager to create the environment that stimulates this kind of productive relationship. This book shows how it can be done.

Throughout the book, there is a constant reference to the "rep." The reader should interpret this term as a reference to the person who represents the company before the customer and prospective customer. Our definition of the word "rep" will be: a company's representative to the ultimate user of a product or service.

FROM
SELLING
TO
MANAGING

1

The Transition From Selling to Managing

Most field sales managers have been salespeople far longer than they have been managers; consequently, the transition from salesperson to manager can be extremely difficult. In fact, many who try never really make the grade. Since this problem occurs so frequently in sales organizations, perhaps it would be well to begin by considering some of the problems involved in making a successful adjustment to the responsibilities of a manager.

As a sales manager, your duties will vary widely from one company to another. Some field sales managers are actually only super-sales reps who handle the more important accounts; some supervise only one or two reps and devote the remainder of their time to direct sales efforts; still others may devote their entire time to supervision and do no direct selling themselves. But all have certain features in common.

The sales rep and the sales manager both deal with people. If you are a sales rep, these people are your prospects and customers. You must be able to influence them, win their confidence and approval. If you are a manager, you must be able to get along with your sales force, win their confidence and respect so that they perform well for you. The sales rep and the sales manager must each be capable of planning the particular activities demanded by their position. Both are, of course, concerned with sales, orders, profits, and their own promotion and advancement. However, it is the critical differences between these two jobs that must be understood if we are to have a sound understanding of the management function.

Five Critical Differences Between Selling and Managing

The first responsibility of sales reps is to *develop accounts*. They must be able to sell accounts in their territory, strengthen the bonds that tie the accounts to the company and to themselves, thus steadily increasing sales volume. As field sales manager, on the other hand, you have one overriding concern—to *develop people—salespeople*. This is by far your chief responsibility. Of course you are concerned about a good sales volume and satisfactory profits, but you cannot achieve these without having developed men and women who can produce that volume and those profits. The moment you step up the line into management you step into the area of responsibility for people, for their growth and development. You are expected to provide the leadership under which your people will produce the sales and profits. Your success no longer depends on your own sales ability but on your capacity to help others to develop and grow in their jobs, to become more skilled and effective, and to perform better as sales reps. Your time, thought, and effort must be directed primarily to the *development of people*. The following interview, in which a sales rep is called into her boss's office and told of the advancement she is about to receive, emphasizes the responsibility of the field sales manager and helps put the position in proper focus. The boss probably said something like this:

> Barbara, you have been brought in here today because we have long recognized the very superior performance you've been turning in. You have increased sales to our most important accounts and have opened many valuable new ones. You have covered your territory in a thorough, systematic manner and have kept your expenses well in line. Your paperwork has always been done promptly and carefully. In short, you have done a top-notch job as a salesperson in your currently assigned territory, and we are about to reward you for this fine performance. A much larger territory will be assigned to you with, of course, the opportunity to earn much more money. Your new territory is so large that you will be unable to cover

it by yourself; you will need the help of a number of people. We consider the entire territory as yours, and we hold you responsible for developing profitable sales from it just as you have been doing in your present territory. Your success will depend upon, and you will be evaluated on, your ability to get your sales force to perform as well as you did as a salesperson. We want to feel that when one of your reps calls upon an account we will be as well represented as if you were there in person. This new assignment is thus a job of *developing the people under you* so that they may become as good as you are.

The second difference is that sales reps perform their jobs by themselves, whereas you perform your job with others. Some of the best salespeople are described as lone wolves because they are interested only in themselves and their own success. They have no feelings for their bosses, the people they work with, or their companies. But they do produce an excellent volume of profitable business. Their customers like them, and no one in the company would recommend the discharge of such a person. They are assets to the companies and to the districts of which they are members. But *not one of them will ever be a manager* because they totally fail to understand the meaning of teamwork.

The third difference is functional. The sales rep is like a player on a football or baseball team, while the manager is like the coach. The manager must develop his player into a team. He does this by winning their loyalty, by making them feel that they are working for a great company, that their products are the very finest, and that company management is tops and really "on the ball." He must see to it that his team members like their fellow workers, respect and look up to their supervisors, and are comfortable with them as people. The sales rep is just an individual with a specific job to do, and can do that job without being part of a team. It is the responsibility of the manager to build a team and to get his salespeople to react as members of a team rather than as individuals working alone.

If the job of the field sales manager could be described with a single word, that word would be *communicator*. Lyndall F. Urwick likens the organization chart of a business to the electrical plan of a large building. Each little block indicating an employee and his or her job is a point through which messages pass like electrical energy. If that post is disconnected, nothing can flow through it in either direction.

The field sales manager manages such a post. It is his function to communicate *down* to his sales reps and, through them, to their prospects and customers on such matters as product and price information, company policies, and the corporate image. He must also communicate *upward* to management concerning customer reaction, competition, acceptance or rejection of any product or line, the reaction of salespeople to company policy and compensation plans, methods of handling orders, and a host of other vital matters. It is inconceivable that top management can do a proper job without good communications between the sales reps and their customers, relaying information to them through the field sales manager. It is equally unlikely that customers and salespeople can be loyal and contented unless communications from the top, through the field sales manager, inform them of the reasoning behind management's decisions and actions.

A fourth and vital distinction between the sales rep and the field sales manager is the fact that unlike the salesperson, *the manager is a part of management.* Their relationship is much the same as that between an officer and an enlisted person in the armed forces. While there must of necessity be warmth and understanding, there must still be recognition that the manager, like the officer, is in command. The manager now *represents management*, and so can no longer make fun of or run down company policies and objectives. Instead, the manager must be able to explain, sell, and implement these policies.

Finally, the contrast between the sales rep and the field sales manager is accentuated by the fact that the field sales manager has a great many more—and diverse—responsibilities. Sales reps have a number of accounts that they are expected to call on, sell, and service. This is their chief and almost sole responsibility. The field sales manager's varied responsibilities may include developing people, recruiting new sales reps, running a branch office, seeing key accounts, handling records, conducting correspondence, and perhaps working with other departments such as advertising, engineering, and credit. Consequently, the field sales manager must know how to organize the work load and use time effectively to a greater extent than is required of the sales rep.

These then are five critical differences between the sales rep and the field sales manager. They demand of the person who moves from the sales force to the first echelon of sales management an entirely new approach to the job and its responsibilities.

The Cycle of Management

To understand the unique problems of sales management as distinct from those of selling, it helps to consider some of the attempts that have been made to define and describe "good management." Among these are the following:

- Good management is the capacity to get people of ordinary ability to perform in an extraordinary manner.
- A good manager is one who can get more work and better performance out of subordinates and get this *willingly*.
- A manager is one who gets things done *through* others or *with* others.

Someone has also said that good managing is *planning* and *controlling*, and out of this definition has grown the concept of the cycle of management. It applies to every person in an organization from the CEO down to the rep in the field. Perhaps it is an oversimplification to say that the cycle of management (Figure 1-1) is a complete definition of management, but when it is coupled with one of the above definitions, it comes mighty close. Let's examine the components of the cycle.

The first step in any management job is to have a plan, but everyone must be in agreement as to what is meant by planning. Many sales managers are frustrated because what they mean by the word "planning" differs from their staff's understanding of the word. To avoid any such confusion, I will explain exactly what I mean by planning.

Planning involves three steps. The first step is to set objectives. The second step is to determine how to reach those objectives. The third step is to decide when the job should be completed.

Most people plan every day of their lives. For example, you sit down with your spouse and say, "Honey, where should we go for our vacation this year?" After discussing a variety of places, you agree that you will drive out to the West Coast and visit the national parks on the way. You set an objective; you complete the first stage of planning. Then you talk over the cost of the trip and ask yourselves whether you can afford it. You decide whether to go by auto, rail, or plane. You decide whether to take the children. This is the second phase of planning. Finally, you decide when you will go, taking into consideration when you can get away from business and

Figure 1-1. The cycle of management.

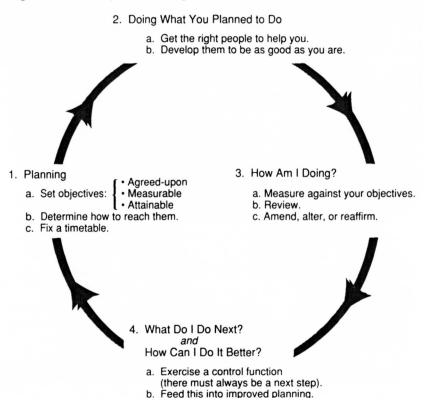

2. Doing What You Planned to Do

    a. Get the right people to help you.
    b. Develop them to be as good as you are.

1. Planning

  a. Set objectives: { • Agreed-upon
                      • Measurable
                      • Attainable
  b. Determine how to reach them.
  c. Fix a timetable.

3. How Am I Doing?

    a. Measure against your objectives.
    b. Review.
    c. Amend, alter, or reaffirm.

4. What Do I Do Next?
        and
How Can I Do It Better?

    a. Exercise a control function
       (there must always be a next step).
    b. Feed this into improved planning.

when you may expect good weather. You are now performing the third phase of the planning function.

With your vacation planned, nothing remains to be done but to carry out the plans you have already made. There is nothing burdensome about all this. It is actually a relief to have completed such a plan, and you experience feelings of satisfaction and pleasurable anticipation. *Planning is a normal function of an orderly mind.*

The next step is to act in accordance with the plan at the appropriate time. Like every field sales manager, you have probably had the following frustrating experience. You've planned an important sales interview with one of your reps. Perhaps you've both spent considerable time reviewing exactly what you were going to say, only to have the sales rep divert the discussion to an entirely different subject immediately upon meeting the prospect. While there are, of course, situations where a plan must be discarded, ordinarily the interview will be far more effective if it has been carefully planned and executed as planned. The same is true of plans for the development of individual sales reps, for the improvement of sales of a certain product line, or for the sale of products to a particular class of trade. Generally, it can be said that once you plan a course of action, you do it—you *carry out the plan!*

The third step in the cycle is to sit back and take a good look at what you have done. You have planned a course of action and implemented your plan with action. Did you accomplish the desired results? What would you do differently if you had to do it all over again? What parts did you do particularly well and in what areas could you have done better? In other words, you make a thorough evaluation of your performance.

This leads directly to the fourth step in the cycle. You have now appraised your performance. Even though you can't turn back the clock, you can learn from the experience. This is perhaps the most important step in the entire cycle—and the one most often omitted. Looking ahead to the next time you will perform this function, you must decide how to make your planning more effective. Your experience, increased knowledge, and careful appraisal of past performance will enable you to make better plans for the next operation. Thus the cycle results in ever-improving performance.

Note that it is impossible to break the cycle and still manage. Management is the complete and continuous repetition of the cycle. Omit any step and you will have confusion instead of management. Applying this cycle to your task as field sales manager, we find that you must (1) determine what you want each of your reps to accomplish; (2) select the most qualified reps and see that the work gets done; (3) check periodically on their performance; and (4) develop methods that will help them to function more effectively. The cycle is equally applicable to the planning for and development of key accounts (see Chapter 2).

Attitude

Having a proper attitude is crucial to being an effective field sales manager. Thinking of yourself as a *helper* is key here. You are not only helping top management to achieve its goals; you are helping your salespeople to carry out the commitments both of you share. This is hard to do if your reps see you only as a "boss."

A boss-underling relationship is a barrier to sound communications. When a salesperson reports to a boss, the inclination is to hide the real problems so as to look as good as possible. By contrast, when the sales rep looks upon the field sales manager as one who needs help and who can offer help in return, as part of a team in getting a common responsibility performed better, the rep is more likely to reveal problems that the field sales manager ought to know about. More comfortable in the presence of this type of field sales manager, the rep is more likely to open up and to discuss problem areas willingly.

There is a great difference between asking "How are *we* doing?" and "How are *you* doing?" The first question implies that the sales rep is part of a team; the second tends to isolate the salesperson, to suggest that his or her problems are purely individual.

There is sometimes the feeling on the part of sales reps that the territory assigned them is a possession and that all others should keep out. The concept of the salesperson as a helper to the field sales manager counteracts this by creating the feeling that the territory belongs to both of them. The "helper attitude" creates a team idea, the idea of two people working together toward a common goal.

When you and your salespeople think of the job as working together, as helping each other to get the job done ever more efficiently and economically; and when the salespeople feel that they are needed helpers and that you listen to them and welcome their input, they will perform at a higher level. They will enjoy their work and feel a sense of responsibility about reaching objectives. In short, there will be a team, a loyal, motivated team.

2

Planning: The First Step

We have established that the first step in sound management is planning. As field sales manager, you have planned well when:

1. You and your supervisor have reached agreed-upon objectives to be attained by a specific date, and have charted a course of action for achieving these objectives.
2. Each of your salespeople, in consultation with you, has agreed-upon objectives to be attained by a specific date and has determined upon a course of action for achieving these objectives.

Of course, you must find out what you are expected to do before you can start planning. How should you go about finding this out?

The Responsibilities of a Sales Manager

Consider the sight of a field sales manager undergoing an annual evaluation. Could this be you? You expected to be patted on the back when you first entered the boss's office, but soon discover that your boss, while crediting you with all your achievements of the past year, has also found a number of shortcomings about which he expresses great concern. You protest: "I didn't *know* I was supposed to do that," or, "How could I tell that you considered this so important?" And your boss replies: "Any fool should have known that this was an important matter to be dealt with." What is the problem in this scenario? It is that there was no written, *agreed-upon* set of objectives established at the beginning of the period by you and your boss. Could you have done anything about it? Yes.

The boss knows what he wants his sales manager to do, but you as sales manager must make sure that you know too. Every field sales manager should have a job description, and it should be in writing. If you do not have one, I suggest that you write a letter to your boss that goes something like this: "Dear Boss, I want very much to succeed in my job and want to be sure that I am doing everything I should be doing. So I have made a list of all the things that I think I should do in order to perform my job well. Will you please go over this list, *delete* what you think should not be there, *add* what I have omitted, *clarify* any statement that you feel is not clear or correct, and then return it to me." This letter and the reply you receive will ordinarily constitute a good job description.

Even this job description may not contain the *specifics* of the manager's job. As we have seen, planning has to do with the setting of specific objectives. This cannot be done until two important steps have been taken. First, you must receive from your supervisor those specific objectives that are part of the company's overall plans. If top management wants greater emphasis put on the sale of a certain product line, then you must be so advised, and this project and its achievement will form a part of your planning. If top management has set a certain minimum increase in sales volume as an objective, you as field sales manager must know what part of that increase you are expected to produce, and this too will become a part of your planning.

Second, as manager you must set objectives with each of the salespeople working under you, and these objectives should be arrived at jointly. When each sales rep has a definite set of agreed-upon objectives, then you can sit down and develop your own plan of action. This will simply be a matter of helping your reps to achieve their own objectives, including for each a share of the manager's load in achieving the company's objectives. Let's now consider how you set objectives with each of your sales reps.

Developing a Plan of Action

There are undoubtedly many methods a field sales manager can use to develop a plan of action. One method may work better for one person than for another. The following method has been found effective when properly employed and is presented as an example of one way of getting this important job done. The procedure is to plan for at least a full day with each sales rep and to work out agreed-upon objectives for that rep's growth and development during the period ahead. The field sales manager must do some preparatory work for such a meeting, and the following steps are suggested as necessary:

1. As sales manager, you should have before you the company objectives you have been given by your supervisor. These may include a dollar quota or unit sales quota for your district that you will then divide up among your force. They may include a directive from top management to give special emphasis to the sale of a specific product line (perhaps a new, large plant has just gone "on stream" and management wants to make sure that its output is sold). Management may also wish to place special emphasis on sales to a particular class of trade it is anxious to penetrate. These company objectives must be discussed with all sales reps so that they know exactly what contribution they are expected to make.

2. Either your own office or the head office must furnish various kinds of statistical material that you and your salespeople will need during the planning session. These data may include such figures as a breakdown of the sales rep's sales for the previous year by product or product lines, by classes of trade, or in other ways; a breakdown of sales and sales effort by accounts, showing for each account the total sales, and sales broken down by product or product lines, the number of calls made by the sales rep on each account, the total number of orders placed by each account, and such other information as may be necessary for a sound planning job with respect to each account. In some companies space is also provided on these sheets for the sales rep's forecast of sales to the account for the period ahead.

3. You must tell your salespeople in advance what is going to take place so they can prepare for it. They too should have a copy of all the statistical material described above; they should also bring to the meeting a diary with space allotted for each day of the period ahead and a card or sheet of paper for each important prospect or customer in the territory regardless of whether they have ever sold the account.

4. As manager you must arrange a place for the planning session. It should be a spot where you will not be disturbed by tele-

phone calls or other interruptions. A hotel room may be the best choice. You should give some thought to the arrangement of the room. For example, if a hotel room is used, each sales rep can sit comfortably at a card table with the work spread out in front; you can be seated away from the table but facing the sales rep so that he or she can participate in an informal and relaxed manner.

5. You should think through carefully how you can develop objectives that will enable you to manage by specifics.

A new term, *management by specifics*, is being injected here, so perhaps I should stop for a moment to define it exactly. For instance, let's assume that your supervisor tells you that top management has decided to make a special effort in the year ahead to sell product line B, and he wants you, through the efforts of your staff, to pull your share of the load in getting sales of this product line. There are at least two ways in which this can be done. One way is for you to call your salespeople together in a district sales meeting and explain to them that management wants an all-out effort made to sell product line B. You review the fine qualities of the line, its advantages to the buyer, its profitability to the company, and perhaps the opportunity for greater earnings by the sales force. You try to work up enthusiasm through a dynamic presentation and send the reps back to their territories with a great big "Go get 'em!" Then, periodically, you check with each to see how they are doing with product line B. This is managing by generalities, and all too often fails to produce results satisfactory to top management.

An alternate method is for you to sit down with each sales rep and, as you review each customer and prospect, ask the specific question:

> Bill, stop and think for a moment. Is there an opportunity to sell product line B to this account? If so, let's list this account on a separate sheet of paper along with others that we decide can be sold this product line.

When this review is finished, the end product will be a mutually agreed-upon list of all the accounts in the sales rep's territory that can buy product line B. Now you will be able to help by calling with the sales rep on some of these accounts, and these calls can be planned in advance.

Using this method, you will know exactly what progress each sales rep is making with the sale of product line B. At any time, you will know how many accounts have been sold this product line, in how many accounts it is under test, what progress is being made toward clinching sales, and exactly which accounts are problems and why. This information will help you to do your job better and will also enable you to give your supervisor an accurate picture of how sales of product line B are coming along in your district and what is being done about it. You are managing by specifics because you know exactly and specifically which accounts can buy product line B in each salesperson's territory and what progress the sales rep is making with each account. With this kind of information you are in a position to "do something about it." If a sales rep is not making headway, you can take appropriate action in time to ensure reaching your objective by the end of the period.

At the very start of the planning session, you should make its purpose clear to the sales rep. This session should *not* deal with such matters as a rep's personal characteristics, a rep's eligibility for a salary increase, or a rep's chances for promotion. A session having to do with the salesperson as an individual should be held at another time. This is important so that sales reps may approach this planning session objectively, in the knowledge that it is intended solely to determine the next steps to be taken in the development of the territory and its important accounts. *Its goal is improved performance by the sales rep.*

Now, having set the stage for the planning session, you are ready to plunge in. The first step is for you and the sales rep to agree upon where the sales rep is right now. You must go over the statistical material that tells what this rep has accomplished during the period just concluded. You should compliment the salesperson who has done well. You should also make a note of those areas in which the sales rep agrees that he or she requires help for further development. You must keep negative remarks out of this session—for example, "You are doing poorly in selling product line B." Instead, you should say,

> Product line B is an area for your further development, and we will want to work together on this.

When you have completed your review of this statistical material with the salesperson and noted in writing any areas for development that have been revealed, the next step can be taken. This is to identify and agree upon the *key accounts*; it involves the whole subject of managing a territory.

Territory Management

The principal concept in good territory management is the effective use of energy and, by extension, concentration on the most productive accounts.

Effective Use of Time

The chief cause of salespeople's failure is their inability to use their time effectively. It has been said that the main difference between a $100,000-a-year sales rep and a $50,000-a-year rep is the way the former uses his time and the speed with which he can make sound decisions. Much of a salesperson's time is spent in (1) conducting interviews with present and prospective customers and (2) going from one interview to another. I am concerned here with the second of these activities.

Territory Management vs. Territory Coverage

The words *territory coverage* suggest geographic coverage of an assigned territory. Salespeople route themselves so as to cover every town along a highway or in a geographic area every time they pass through this section. In some companies this procedure is described as a "combing" operation.

In businesses such as those selling to supermarkets and chain stores, this may be thought desirable because of the need to service each store. It is doubtful, however, even in these cases, that such mechanical coverage is the best procedure. Generally, it is not profitable to have a sales rep "cover a territory" if that means routing is plotted without regard to any factor except geography. It used to be said that there were two kinds of men "on the road"—traveling men and salesmen. Most companies want their force in the field to sell.

The Concept of Account Development

What, then, should salespeople be doing? Briefly stated, the job of a sales rep is to develop accounts. This is not a case of simply selling to accounts but of selling to them in such a manner that they may be sold to repeatedly and, in the process, of strengthening the loyalty of the account to the sales rep and company and increasing the volume of business from the account or perhaps selling it additional product lines. In short, *only accounts capable of development are "worthwhile" or key.* (An exception to this statement is the occasional large but nonrecurring transaction—for example, a big government contract.) *In most territories, 80 percent of the potential lies with about 20 percent of the accounts.* Sales reps who can secure the business of this 20 percent have it made. Therefore, this 20 percent must be identified and the major sales effort made with them, and the major servicing of accounts must be with them, too. The field sales manager must be involved with the salesperson in this effort, namely in setting the objectives for the development of the account, in helping to solve problems that arise, and, in an emergency, being able to step in and take over. If the sales rep is to be successful, the major effort must be expended on those accounts that have the greatest potential for development.

A prospective buyer must reach five major conclusions regarding a company's salesperson before deciding to do business with that company or to continue doing business with it. It may take quite a while before these five elements crystallize in the buyer's mind but, when they do, the sales rep and the company have a good customer. The process is as follows:

1. The customer comes to like the sales rep and is always glad to see and talk with him or her.
2. The customer trusts that the sales rep will never oversell or misrepresent anything.
3. The customer concludes that the salesperson is better informed about his products than any of his competitors are about theirs. He obviously knows his business.
4. The customer concludes that the sales rep understands *his* problems and can help to solve them.
5. The customer believes that the salesperson has the backing of a solid company that will stand behind its products.

It is the basic job of the sales rep to make the customer think in this way. No one else can bring it about. To accomplish this, the rep must spend a great deal of time in servicing the account even though this is a very expensive procedure. Such service can only be given profitably to companies whose potential volume of business is large enough to warrant it. It cannot be given to every account equally. Salespeople once thought that they had to give this kind of service across the board; however, investment counselors, attorneys, accountants, advertising agencies, and others have long given service to accounts in proportion to each account's profitability. At this point, a definition is in order. *A "worthwhile" or key account is any account whose volume of purchases and profitability on a continuing basis is large enough to justify the salesperson's rendering a degree of service greater than that given by any competitor.* To sum up then, the sales rep's first job, in trying to cover the territory effectively, is to identify these key accounts, separate them, and plan the territorial coverage around them.

Planning Territorial Coverage Around Key Accounts

There are many ways to plan territorial coverage around key accounts, but let's first examine one method in detail. The steps are as follows:

1. Obtain a map of the assigned geographical territory.

2. With a marking crayon, place a dot where each of the key accounts is located. Note that these accounts will usually be found in clusters.

3. Draw a circle around each cluster and number each circle as a zone. Thus each zone is formed by a cluster of key accounts.

4. Compare the number of key accounts in any one zone with the number in other zones. For example, assume that, out of a total of one hundred worthwhile accounts in the entire territory, there are forty such accounts in Zone 1, twenty in Zone 2, ten in Zone 3, twenty in Zone 4, and ten in Zone 5. Figure 2-1 illustrates just such a clustering.

5. Obtain a diary, and for the current year (using a pencil so that changes can be made when necessary) mark a zone number next to each working day of the year in such a manner that the proportion of days spent in each zone reflects the relative number of key accounts in each (see Figure 2-2). In the example used here, out of every one hundred working days during the year, the sales rep would assign forty days to Zone 1, twenty days each to Zones 2 and 4, and ten days each to Zones 3 and 5.

6. Write the name of each of the one hundred key accounts in the diary just once, indicating the time when the next call is to be made. This diary entry will alert the sales rep to prepare adequately for the forthcoming interview.

Figure 2-1. A cluster of key accounts showing the density in each of five zones.

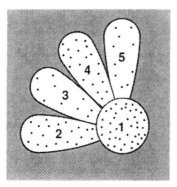 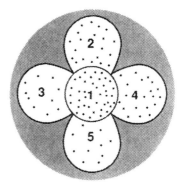

Legend: Zone 1—40 key accounts
2—20 "   "
3—10 "   "
4—20 "   "
5—10 "   "

For every day spent in either Zone 3 or Zone 5 the sales rep should spend 2 days in Zone 2 or Zone 4 and 4 days in Zone 1. This need not be done consecutively, but over a period of time this ratio of time will generally prevail. The sketch at left illustrates a territory like the fingers of a hand. This is usually a more extensive territory or a rural territory where it would not be convenient to cross from one territory to another. The sketch at the right illustrates a more urban territory , condensed, more easily traversed .

7. Immediately after the interview, when your knowledge is fresh, determine when the next call should be made on this customer and why. Then plan the next call and enter its date into the diary. Under some circumstances, the sales rep and the prospect or customer may have agreed upon a date for this next call, which ideally should coincide with a day the rep was planning to be in that particular zone.

8. Never make calls mechanically at regular intervals but only when there is a reason for making the call—a reason that furthers the development of the account. Actually, an account may be called upon forty times one year and only six times the following year, depending on the development work necessary. At the beginning of the year, nobody knows how often any given account should be called upon. Only the calls themselves reveal the desired course of action to be taken by the sales rep and the optimum frequency of contact with the account.

Figure 2-2. Example of a sales rep's diary with the days marked by zone.

WEEK OF FEBRUARY 17

Monday, February 17   (Zone 1)

9	1
10	2
11	3
12	4

Tuesday, February 18   (Zone 1)

9	1
10	2
11	3
12	4

Wednesday, February 19   (Zone 2)

9	1
10	2
11	3
12	4

Handling the Smaller Accounts

In every territory there are a number of smaller accounts whose aggregate business constitutes perhaps 20 percent of its total sales. This volume of business is not to be overlooked. When sales reps learn from their diaries that they may have some time free between calls on key accounts, they should prepare a list of smaller accounts located in the same zone so that they may call upon as many of these as time will allow. In this way they can maintain contact with these smaller accounts. In addition, they can use the telephone to talk with them even when they cannot see them in person. These smaller accounts do not expect to be called upon as frequently as larger accounts and will often appreciate a phone call as much as a personal call.

Calling on Key Accounts to Further a Sales Strategy

Sales reps must always have a carefully planned strategy for the development of every key account in their territory. In carrying out this strategy they must deploy their time so that contacts with the account are made only when they expect to take some specific action to advance their development of the account. Above all, they must know the optimum time to make the call. *They must be where the business is when it is going to be placed*. This includes not only the final transaction but also the preliminaries leading up to it. Sales reps must avoid calling too early to close the deal, thus necessitating an additional call a week or two later. And they certainly will not want to arrive too late and find that the business has been placed elsewhere. Good planning tells them when the customer is ready to take action and signals when they should be there to make sure that the action is favorable to them and their company.

The old-fashioned way of requiring salespeople to follow routes predetermined by their supervisors tends to make coverage of the territory mechanical. It also retards personal development by letting the boss or the home office do the thinking they should be doing—or perhaps nobody is doing any really sound planning for territorial coverage. The method suggested here motivates sales reps by giving them a true sense of responsibility for the effective use of their time. Thus it makes better-thinking, better-performing salespeople of them. Territorial coverage is a tool they *they* use to improve their performance. When this method is taught and used properly, the company not only gets more effective coverage of the important accounts, with a resultant increase in sales, but better salespeople are developed; employees who are happier, more confident, and certainly more successful.

Improving the Sales Rep's Ability to Plan Account Development

The sales rep and the field sales manager must plan in depth for the development of each of the important or key accounts. Here is one suggested way of doing this. The important accounts are arranged alphabetically by cities and by name of the account under each city. The first account is selected, and the field sales manager begins to ask the sales rep questions about the account. The ques-

tions may be varied, but all have the same objective—to develop a comprehensive plan or strategy for the development of that account.
The questions will run along the following lines:

- What have we done with this account up to now?
- What items do we sell them and how much of each?
- Are we supplying the total requirements of this company? If not, what percentage of its business are we now obtaining? How can we increase this amount?
- What are the chief problems that we are helping this company to solve with our product(s)?
- In what other areas can we serve the company?
- Which of its people do we now deal with? Are these the decision-making authorities? If not, how can we reach the decision-making authorities so that they can hear our story at first hand?
- What obstacles stand in the way of our complete development of this account and what can we do about them?
- What do you regard as the next step to be taken in the development of this account? When do you expect to take it? Can you estimate the volume of business to be secured from this account during the next period?
- Do you believe that this account is a potential purchaser of product line B and, if so, how do you propose going about selling it to them?

These questions are posed in a conversational manner, and time should be allowed for frank discussion between the sales rep and the manager sharing in the planning. This is not a quiz. It is *a mental exercise designed primarily to stimulate and improve the thinking of the sales rep so that it results in a plan of action for the development of each account.* The results are (1) the setting of objectives for the development of the account; (2) a determination as to how to reach those objectives; and (3) the setting of a date when the first step will be taken.

The sales rep keeps a record of his plan for the development of each account. He enters on the customer card or sheet the agreed-upon objectives for the development of the account and the notes that grew out of his discussion with his manager on how to achieve these objectives (see Figures 2-3 and 2-4). When the final notations have been made on the customer's sheet or cards and in the diary, the sales rep and his manager are ready to proceed to the next account.

(text continues on page 24)

Figure 2-3. A prospect record card with notes indicating action to be taken in developing the account.

Acme Manufacturing Company, Attleboro   Zone 1

Sam Smith, P.A.
John Jones, M.M. *daughter was sick*
Mack Brown, Chf. Engr.
Bill Evers, Supt.

Product "B" in Plant 4 (see Evers)
Would lower Material Handling Costs
Cultivate Brown –
Lower labor costs thru use of Prod A (see Jones)
– Take Jones to G.E. Plant installation

Figure 2-4. A prospect record card containing personal information regarding large key accounts.

Key Buying Influences

Name:

Title:

Personal background (age, likes, education, positions in company):

Years with company:

Reports to:

Possible next job:

Who will replace him/her?

First called on when, by whom:

3M executive—management when, by whom:

(continues)

Figure 2–4. (cont.)

Visits to 3M facilities, where, when, whom:

Attitude toward 3M:

Relationship in company to other KBIs and/or sphere of influence:

Buying influencer: End User [   ] Evaluator [   ] Adviser [   ]
                     Financial [   ] Mover [   ]

Percentage of buying influence:
Style:
Personal wants, needs, goals:

My relationship:

My goal for improvement:

Trust is the relationship upon which all lasting business relations are built.

Other Buying Influences

Name: _____

Title: _____

Personal background (age, likes, education, positions in company):

_____

_____

Years with company: _____

Reports to: _____

Figure 2-4. (cont.)

Possible next job: _____

Who will replace him/her? _____

Relationship in company to other KBIs and/or sphere of influence:

_____

_____

Type: _____

Style: _____

Personal, wants, needs, goals: _____

My relationship: _____

Other: _____

_____

_____

Name: _____

Title: _____

Personal background (age, likes, dislikes, education, positions in company): _____

_____

_____

Years with company: _____

Reports to: _____

Possible next job: _____

Who will replace him/her? _____

Relationship in company to other KBIs and/or spheres of influence:

_____

_____

Type: _____

Style: _____

Personal, wants, needs, goals: _____

My relationship: _____

Other: _____

_____

_____

Trust is the relationship upon which all lasting business relations are built.

Note particularly how the field sales manager ties in with this planning his own and company plans involving the sales of product line B. When this technique is employed in a sound manner, experience has proved that after some twenty accounts have been reviewed in this manner, the sales rep begins to "take over" the questioning and to apply the questioning process to each account without waiting for the field sales manager to ask the questions. This is exactly the desired result of this procedure. It is an indication that the sales rep is learning to think in a sound and constructive manner about the accounts and their development.

Now the sales rep has a plan of action for every key account in his territory. The rep not only knows *what* must be done, but *how* to do the job, and *when* to take the first step. In addition, there is a list of accounts, good potential customers for product line B. Finally, the sales rep and the field sales manager have agreed on what it is that the rep must do to develop himself during the coming year.

Let's look at this question of development from the manager's point of view. Since it is your primary responsibility as field sales manager to develop the sales force, it is important that you and each sales rep agree on the nature and means of achieving this objective so that the rep can work at it when you are not present. Therefore, upon the conclusion of a developmental session, you should prepare a written list of a few major objectives that the rep can refer to and work from throughout the year ahead (see Figure 2-5). For instance, one obvious objective will be the quota or sales goal. A second objective will be to increase the sales of product line B, because this is a company objective. It may be found during this session that one of the sales rep's major problems is an inability to get to the real decision-making authorities. Solution of this problem should be noted as an agreed-upon objective. Thus there are, in this case, three major objectives to be achieved by the sales rep.

The sales rep now knows what his job is and can proceed to the second phase of the cycle of management—doing it. And you as field sales manager know exactly what your job is with respect to this rep—that is, to help him stay on track and keep to the plans he has made, to help him achieve his objectives with his important accounts, to help him get the product line B business he has committed himself to getting, and to help him learn how to reach the decision-making people in the firms he calls on. This is quite a task for any field sales manager, and it will require all your knowledge and experience to perform the function skillfully and finish the year with a better, more seasoned, and more valuable sales rep.

Figure 2-5. List of a sales rep's developmental objectives.

Objectives for
(199–)

For: Phil Smith

Agreed upon:
January 19, 199—

1. Increase sales of product
   line B
   Jones Mfg. Co.
   Ajax Mfg. Co.
   Perfection Drill
   Perkins Instrument
   Marvel Plow
   McPherson Corp.
   All-Test Products

2. Increase sales to class of
   trade 6
   Philpott Industries
   Masterson Corp.
   Baker and Weston Inc.
   Best Company
   Anchor Products

3. Get to decision-making au-
   thorities
   Nicholson Co.
   Obermeyer and Smith Corp.
   Smithville Mfg. Co.
   Carbide
   Hooker

4. Dollar volume to exceed $___

5. Improve planning of each sales
   interview.

For the individual sales rep the developmental process accomplishes at least two very important things:

1. With respect to the accounts that can provide 80 percent of the territorial potential, he has a carefully thought out plan that will bring him to each of those accounts at the optimum time.
2. He knows exactly what to do when he gets to the account. He has planned a sound interview that will enable him to be much more effective when he approaches the prospective buyer.

Both these functions can be supervised by the field sales manager. Observation of the sales rep's performance by the sales manager in the field can be instrumental in improving that rep's capabilities.

The Field Sales Manager's Function With Respect to Distributors

Many organizations in addition to having full-time sales representatives also have distributors to sell and service their customers. In many instances, the immediate responsibility for the development of the distributor rests with the salesperson. The role of the field sales manager is a bit more complex.

The pluses of having a distributorship can be summarized as follows:

- The distributor usually knows the buyers of suppliers' products or services. They are friends of his. He sells them other things. Their door is always open to the distributor. Distributors make it easier to break into the market.
- The distributor usually carries a stock of your products and parts necessary for the quick servicing of customers and is a ready source of information and servicing.
- The distributor can extend credit to smaller accounts whose aggregate volume may be of value to the supplier.

On the other hand, the distributor who handles a wide range of products lacks the time or ability to aggressively court new accounts and to expand the business within the assigned area. Also, in many cases, the supplier would prefer to perform the entire distribution function. Often, the distributor is dispensed with when the volume of business in an area becomes large enough to support the supplier's performing all the services. The distributor knows this very well. This can create a barrier between the supplier and distributor. The distributor does not want the supplier to know who the buyers are because of the fear that the supplier may some day take the business away.

Obviously, such a barrier is a great obstacle to the sound development of the area being served. The supplier is really running blind. He does not know the extent of the available business; does not know whether important new accounts are being opened; does not know brand and company acceptance by customers or the degree of acceptance of competitors' products in the marketplace; and does not know whether accounts are really being serviced in a constructive manner.

As a field sales manager, your first responsibility is to know and understand the policy of your employer respecting distributors and to convey this policy clearly to the distributor as a step in breaking down barriers. Getting the distributor to see himself as part of the supplier's sales organization rather than as a customer of the supplier, and to think of the customer as the person or organization to whom the distributor sells, is what you want to accomplish.

At least once a year, you, the sales rep, and the distributor should jointly develop agreed-upon objectives that will then serve as the basis for working together and for appraising performance.

The salesperson has the direct responsibility for working with the distributor to achieve objectives. The rep and the distributor will, through personal contacts with key accounts, jointly develop new accounts and stimulate the growth of established accounts. But as field sales manager, you are responsible for making sure that the sales rep and the distributor perform in this manner. The salesperson must be the chief channel through which the distributor remains in contact with the company. Yet, you too must maintain personal contact with the distributor on a continuing and regular basis, though always with the salesperson present.

Through your training and development of the sales rep, you must make sure that the distributor maintains an inventory adequate to service accounts, that assistance of a technical nature is provided when requested, that complaints and other problems are handled promptly, that new products are introduced and promoted, and that important key accounts are developed so that they grow steadily and strengthen in loyalty.

When important business is pending, you must be available to the distributor to work with the account. As field sales manager, you should work to train and develop the distributor just as you have worked steadily with your sales reps to improve their performance.

Dealing With Dealers Who Sell
Directly to the Consumer

The key accounts in this area are usually those with retail outlets, and there is no best way to proceed with them. One way is for the field sales manager to contact the central or area buying group of the account and succeed in having his company's products and services accepted. The sales rep can then contact the individual store manager and the department manager to obtain their order. This order may be an assignment of space to be filled. The salesperson is thus responsible for seeing that the space is filled with products that are selling and that there is an additional supply in the back of the store. The sales rep calls at the store at pretty fixed intervals. In some cases, the main office computerizes the scheduling of the salesperson's time. The salesperson is also responsible for adding products and for obtaining permission to put the company product in special and advantageous locations at special times of the year (like placing a sage dressing next to the turkeys at Thanksgiving). All these tasks will be supervised by the field sales manager.

Organization and Manpower Planning

After you have completed the planning sessions with your sales reps, you should be in a position to do some fairly accurate estimating with regard to (1) your staffing requirements and (2) the potential of your entire district or region in terms of sales volume.

Estimating Staffing Requirements

First, take a good look at each of your people. Are they all really capable of development—good material to work with? If the answer is negative, then determine the following:

- Should the rep be replaced as soon as possible?
- Should he or she be retired if at or near retirement age and then replaced?
- When age or ill health is an issue, should the rep be assigned a smaller territory or certain special accounts, thus leaving most of the present territory available for another or a more junior rep?
- Should a rep's territory be divided because of its unusual growth or because, for some other reason, the rep is not capable of properly covering all the important accounts?
- Should a rep be transferred or reassigned, thus leaving this territory open?

With this information you can determine how many new sales reps you will need during the year ahead and can requisition them so that you will be fully staffed to meet the objectives and goals you have accepted.

Estimating Market Potential

Projecting sales volume can best be done in conjunction with the sales rep in each territory. The rep often knows more about the accounts in a particular territory than anybody else in the company, and in any event probably has a good feel for their potential. The following steps can be helpful:

1. Estimate with the sales rep the potential for every key account in that rep's territory. The total, with something additional for smaller accounts, will be a fair estimate of the potential for the territory as a whole. Include potentials for accounts *not* sold as well as for accounts that have been sold.
2. Add up the various territorial potentials within the district, including territories not presently assigned. This sum will equal the total potential of the entire district or region.

This information can be helpful in:

- Setting district or regional sales quotas with your boss.
- Determining the need to split a territory or to add more territory to a sales rep's assignment.
- Determining the degree to which the company is handicapped by salespeople who, because of advanced age, illness, or some other reason, are not coming close to realizing the full potential of the territory. This may make it easier for management to reach agreement with you as to what steps are to be taken to correct the situation.
- Determining the need for additional salespeople within your assigned territory.

Forecasting Sales and Staffing Requirements at the Field Sales Manager's Level

The very word *forecast* sends a shudder through anyone who spends time out in the field selling or teaching others how to sell. After all, the person in the field is not a technical genius and wasn't hired as one. In some companies the field sales manager, as a member of the first sales management echelon, is not asked to do any forecasting. It is all done back at headquarters. This often makes the manager unhappy, but probably not as unhappy as trying to do the job alone. In other companies, even though the job of forecasting is done at headquarters, the field sales manager is also involved by being requested to send in his own forecast. As we have seen, field managers who are required to do this often obtain estimates from their sales reps to assist them in arriving at their figures.

It is not uncommon for forecasting to begin at the bottom of an organization and end up at the very top, where the information is digested, reviewed, and reworked into the final form acceptable to top management. Then it filters back down through the entire organization to the very bottom. Such a process usually results in greater acceptance of final forecasts by the sales personnel charged with achieving the goals set by the forecasts and facilitates the attainment of these objectives. And often such forecasts are more realistic than would be the case were they initiated at the top.

How can you as a field sales manager do a good forecasting job? Let's fall back again on a single example that will provide food for thought and help you to develop a method best suited to your operations. In practice, the job of forecasting is often tied in very closely with the annual planning session. As you and the sales rep consider each key account, you ask the rep to estimate the volume of business he or she will secure from the account in the year ahead, and also to estimate the potential of that account. This is written down next to the name of the account. The total of the estimates for each account is the estimate or forecast of the sales that all the key accounts will produce during the period in question. If these key accounts provide about 80 percent of all the business, then you and your sales rep may add 25 percent to this figure to get a fair forecast for the entire territory. Experience has shown that while sales reps may not be very accurate as forecasters at first, they will become quite proficient by the end of three years. Frequently, a rep's forecast will be as reliable as one produced by the research people back at headquarters, and occasionally even more accurate. Much depends on the nature of the business; some businesses can measure potential sales with great accuracy; others must do some pretty fancy guessing to make a forecast.

The forecast just described concerns only one territory covered by a particular salesperson. The same territory may produce more or less business depending on who the sales rep is at any given time. The full potential will remain the same regardless of the sales rep. As field sales manager you must consider this in arriving at your forecast for the entire district. As you go through planning sessions with one after another of your people, you add the forecasts together, eventually arriving at a total that represents the amount of business you can realistically expect to obtain for your company in the year ahead. To this figure you must add your estimate of any sales for which you are personally responsible and of such business as you expect to get from territories now unassigned but for which you anticipate finding sales reps during the year ahead. You will increase this by any probable rise in sales resulting from the replacement of below-average sales reps with others from whom you expect better results.

After the planning sessions, you consider each rep's strengths and weaknesses and evaluate their potential. What does all this have to do with forecasting and staffing development? Simply this. The sales rep may reach a point in the planning session where he throws up his hands and says: "I don't have enough time. There are more accounts here than I can develop in the way they deserve." As manager, you may properly suggest at this point that perhaps the territory has become too large and should be subdivided. You may ask the rep to help you find a way to do this that will be fair both to the present sales rep and to the new salesperson.

When sales reps themselves recognize the need for subdividing a territory, it can be done better and without impairing morale. One of the serious mistakes made by sales management in subdividing a territory is to fail to consult the incumbent salesperson. It has repeatedly been found that involvement of the sales rep in planning a subdivision of the territory gets better results and avoids bad feelings. It is a form of recognition that will mitigate any feeling the sales rep might have of being deprived of something.

This brings up another point. Some salespeople actually feel that the territory and the accounts are their personal property. As manager, you must quickly correct this misconception. The territory and the accounts in it are the company's. The company has divided its area of operations among various field sales managers who in turn have divided their areas and accounts among sales reps who in essence are their helpers. The sales rep may have done a fine job of building up the assigned territory, but you must make this salesperson aware that his or her success could not have been achieved without the help of effective sales management or without the backing of a reliable company with sound policies and quality products.

At least once a year you should take a long look at each of your people to determine what you must do during the year ahead to strengthen the staffing of your district or region. For those who are capable of development, you will set agreed-upon objectives. For others, you will have to decide whether to fire them. You will have to appraise the older reps objectively and see which will be retiring and should be replaced soon and which should have some adjustments made in their assignments to enable them to continue work but at a reduced pace. This may result in a decision to bring in another sales rep.

Good field sales managers can be especially effective in meeting the various problems discussed here. But they must be capable of the kind of basic thinking about the job that leads to the right decisions in such matters as planning, forecasting, and forwarding the development of the salespeople in their charge. Their skill in these matters will grow with the years.

3

Implementing the Plan

Let's now move on to the next major step—implementing the plan. As field sales manager you perform this part of the job when:

1. You have the right salespeople to do the job.
2. You supervise these reps to make sure they are reaching their agreed-upon objectives.

In short, what we have is a plan of action for each sales rep working under the field sales manager. These individual plans also include specific steps for achieving the company's overall objectives. In our hypothetical case, each sales rep has a specific plan for increasing the sales of product line B as well as for attaining additional objectives agreed upon for his or her individual growth and development. *The field sales manager's own plan of action is to help each sales rep achieve objectives.*

This job is done largely in the field. Ordinarily, *those* field sales managers with ten reps under them find it necessary to spend from 60 to 80 percent of their time in the field with their reps. To do this, they must keep office work to a minimum and learn how to handle it with maximum efficiency. Figure 3-1 is an example of a typical sales manager's time allocation sheet.

Basically, your job as manager is to improve the thinking of your people because they usually perform alone. It is a rare occasion when you are with them on their calls. It is therefore essential to get them to perform well in your absence. To do so, your salespeople must be thinking along the same lines. Implied in the achievement

Figure 3-1. Field coaching: time allocation sheet.

Field Coaching: Time Allocation Sheet

A. Need determines the *balance* in the amount of time spent with each of your reps. List their names and give each a need priority number.

B. Next determine the percent of time you will spend in Field Coaching.

100%   90%   80%   70%   60%   50%

C. How many days will you have available.

230 Work Days Per Year

$$\frac{\text{230 Work Days Per Year}}{\text{% of Time You Will Spend In the Field}} = \text{Total Days Available for Field Work}$$

D.

$$\frac{\text{Total Days Available for Field Work}}{\text{Total Number of Reps}} = \text{Average Field Work Days Per Rep}$$

Name of Rep	Priority Number	Avg. Days	Total Days	Days I Will Work This Year/Quarter			
				1st	2nd	3rd	4th

of this goal is a recognition that as a manager *you will never get anywhere until you make your reps want to change their habits and improve their thinking.*

Another important concept is that field contacts between you and your sales force must have continuity. Each must be related to the previous one and to the one that will inevitably follow. The field contacts must be a series of efforts on your part that build toward specific goals and objectives which are known, agreed upon, and in writing. *Each field contact builds upon the previous one.* All too often field sales managers conduct "flying contacts" with their people, rushing to see them without any specific plan, spending their time on visits to important accounts and calls to help close some big business deal for the sales rep or to straighten out complaints of important customers. The individual rep is often relieved when the visit is over, and the field sales manager is equally happy to return to his desk and the mountain of paperwork he will find on it. Since I wish to change this version of the field contact to the kind of visit described in the opening sentences of this paragraph, I recognize that some careful planning is necessary before making a field contact with a sales rep.

It may be well at this point to clarify exactly what ought to be accomplished in this proposed series of field contacts. In your planning sessions with each of your reps you have mutually agreed on *what* each is to do to achieve the objectives that have been set. There remains the question: Do they know *how* to do it? *Showing them how to do the job is also the field sales manager's responsibility.*

The field contact has additional goals, which must also be kept in mind. One of these is the reduction of staff turnover. Sales reps who might otherwise become discouraged and leave for another job are stimulated by field contacts to become valuable members of the team. The manager's field work with the salespeople will improve their performance. As they become more productive sales reps, they feel more secure in the job, take greater satisfaction in their work, and often strive for promotion. Thus the field contact, when properly planned and performed, can do wonders. *No report can give so accurate a picture of the performance of sales reps as may be obtained by seeing them in action with a customer.* Their strengths and weaknesses become apparent, and the latter can be more easily corrected when they are encouraged with commendation for any progress they have made.

Changing Habits

It may appear that field contacts are being overemphasized in these pages. However, they deserve the attention I have given them. What you are actually attempting to do for them is to change many established habits of your sales reps. You say to them, in effect: "Stop doing it *that* way and start doing it *this* way." Even after your salespeople accept your point of view and want to follow your directions, they are in for a very difficult time. Why? Anyone who has ever tried to stop smoking or follow a diet knows how difficult it is to change fixed habits. Efforts to break habits fail far more frequently than they succeed. We have all heard: "This one cigarette won't hurt me," or, "I'll just taste a little of the apple pie; I'll be back on my diet in the morning." These remarks usually signal the defeat of an effort to alter a habit. Well, the same thing happens with salespeople. They start out with every intention of doing what you recommend. Then, after a week or two of working alone in the field, their determination weakens and they revert to their old habitual ways of doing things. Unless they are caught up promptly and made to do things properly, it will become extremely difficult—if not impossible—to start them on the right path again. You have probably used your most powerful ammunition to sell them on making the original commitment to improve their habits. You have little left to inspire them now.

The alert field sales manager expects backsliding and watches for it. When it appears, he immediately goes out into the field to correct the erring sales rep. Consequently, the interval between the rep's reversion to bad habits widens after each such field contact. Eventually the habit is changed; the field sales manager has accomplished this particular task, and is free to move on to other efforts to improve the rep's performance. The foregoing discussion should make it clear to you as a field sales manager that your job must be done primarily in the field and cannot possibly be performed from behind a desk, no matter how many reports and statistics you may have at your disposal.

Planning the Field Contact

Detailed planning is vitally important if the field contact is to be a fruitful experience for the field sales manager and the sales rep. The field contact must be planned jointly by both of them. It is important for each to know what the other hopes to accomplish from the meeting; consequently, ample time for planning must be allowed. A minimum of two weeks is suggested unless there is some emergency. Here are some of the important steps to be taken by the field sales manager in crystallizing plans:

1. Review the agreed-upon objectives arrived at during the planning session. Determine which of these you wish to help the sales rep with during the forthcoming contact.

2. Study the sales rep's past performance to determine where she could use some help, additional training, counseling, or coaching.

3. If you have a file for the sales rep, go over it for any notes or correspondence that might reveal subjects worth discussing or areas where you can assist in developing the rep.

4. Determine whether there are any special situations requiring your help, like closing business deals or strengthening relationships with important accounts.

5. Check with headquarters for any problems or other matters that you can deal with effectively during a field contact. These might include credit difficulties or situations involving the engineering, advertising, or sales research departments.

6. Determine what equipment you will take with you. For instance, you may wish to help the sales rep improve her sales of product line B. Do not depend upon her to have all the necessary sales tools for an effective effort to sell or promote this product line. She may inadvertently leave some of this material at home on the day you are scheduled to meet, or her equipment may be in poor condition. Bring all this equipment with you in case it is needed to demonstrate the value of this product line.

7. From all of the foregoing you can judge the probable length of the field contact.

8. Now are you ready to write your sales rep a letter setting forth the date and estimated length of the contact. You should also state the time you will arrive, the time and place of the projected meeting, and specifically what you would like to accomplish. This letter will tell her what she must do to prepare for the contact. For instance, you may ask her to plan at least two calls on accounts

which, she has agreed, are prospects for product line B and on two accounts where she has had difficulty in getting a hearing from the decision-making authorities.

9. Finally, bring her into the planning of the field contact by asking her whether there are any specific calls she wishes to make with you or any specific matters she wishes to discuss with you so that you can be prepared to handle these matters effectively when you are with her. It is important for the sales rep to understand that you are giving her an opportunity to prepare for your contact with her and that she owes you the same consideration—that is, an opportunity to prepare to discuss matters that concern her and that she wants to resolve while you are there. It is suggested that you refuse to discuss any matters of which she has failed to give you advance notice. She must realize that it is unfair to "hit you cold" with gripes when you are with her. By giving you prior notice of such matters, she gives you an opportunity to obtain information from the home office or otherwise prepare to resolve the problem.

10. When her reply arrives, you can then fit her requests into the schedule for the field contact and write a final letter setting forth the completed plans so that she can make the necessary arrangements in advance to ensure a profitable experience for both of you. Now everything is set for the field contact.

Figure 3-2, a reprint of a 3M brochure on presession analysis and planning, gives further insight into how to go about planning.

The Field Contact

The first step is to "clear the decks." By this I mean that you first dispose of those matters that are worrying the sales rep. A rep cannot be expected to absorb the developmental training you have planned while emotionally or mentally disturbed about some situation. If the contact is to be effective, the rep must be ready to learn.

A sales rep may carry some gripe in his breast for hours until the field sales manager finally gives him an opportunity to talk it out. Often this is at the end of the day, just before the manager dashes away to the airport. The field sales manager in such a situation may not recognize that he has wasted the entire day simply because the sales rep was preoccupied with his gripe and hence unable to absorb the valuable help provided by the manager. Yet the

(text continues on page 42)

Figure 3-2. Example of a presession analysis and planning reminder.

1. Pre-Session Analysis and Planning

A. Setting Up the Coaching Session

Determine the objective—Consult your coaching folder. Consider readiness level for each task and appropriate leadership style. Review results of previous coaching sessions. Consider needs, past and present performance. Motivational profile.

Example

Distributor Business Review—Owner—Mgt.

Cold Calls—Specific product—Promotion

Key Account Calls—Top Level Presentation

Distributor Sales Meeting

Nite Demo

Difficult Account—Situation— Be the "Fall Guy"

Account Just Sold—Case study for other reps

Account Card Review

No Objective—Field Work— Leave it up to the rep

Ask them beforehand how you can be of most value

Key Account Review

Team effort to close a sale

½ Day—Telephone Appointments—Qualifying

Review their time & territory plans for the next quarter— 30 days

Provide time, date, location. How much advance notice? Meet early in the field—not the office.

The rep may have many things to discuss with you. Prioritize. Don't let these things overshadow your coaching objectives, based on the needs of the rep.

(continues)

Figure 3–2. (cont.)

B. Meeting the Rep

Set the tone, mood, pace for the coaching session—high expectations —self-fulfilling prophecy.

Establish objectives for the day(s). Compliment on past performance. A person must feel good about themselves before change can take place. Emphasize self-improvement, self-development. Let them know how they are getting along, where they stand, what's expected.

Prepare for the field coaching session as you would for a call on a "Key Account." Consider their feelings, put yourself in their shoes, consider the rejection they face.

How you set up the field coaching session will, to a large degree determine the rep's receptivity to your coaching and attitude to his/her self improvement and future behavior after the coaching session.

Confidence, respect for one another, trust are the foundations for leadership.

C. Preparing the Rep Before the Call

Build up his/her self respect— confidence, pride, remind them of another similar important sale they have recently made.

Have them use the pre-call planning sheet on important calls. For new reps, help them to fill it out and rehearse before the call. Help them anticipate objections before the call & overcome them before they are raised.

Encourage them to look and ask for applications for other 3M products & services and turn over leads, cooperation for growth.

Help make them feel they belong to a team.

Urge them to come out of their "comfort zone" to take some risks to grow and achieve greater accomplishments.

Ask how you can help—or gain support from head office staff— literature spec's, etc.

Encourage innovation, initiative, creativity in the call.

Review ground rules as to what involvement you will take in the call, if any.

Pick up the bag, make some cold calls yourself—let the rep analyze your calls.

Observe what the rep does in his/her waiting time.

(continues)

Figure 3-2. (cont.)

Objective Worksheet

Objectives should be specific, measurable, attainable, with stretch. (Regular, problem solving, innovative, personal)				Specific plans and methods to achieve objectives	Accomplishment Date
"To	(verb)	(end result)	(subject)	(time)"		

Form 10194-1-A

Reprinted with permission from the 3M Corporation, St. Paul, Minnesota.

day probably was a total loss. It was a very costly one, too, because the instruction was lost, the time of the manager and of the sales rep was lost, the dollar cost of the day was lost, and, above all, an important opportunity to build a sounder relationship between the rep and the field sales manager was missed.

Is it not better to sit down with the sales rep *first* and resolve any matters that concern him? Regardless of whether this is done at the airport, in the hotel, or in the sales rep's car, it is an important first step in any field contact. It is important to bring incipient troubles to the surface before they become crises or serious problems. This is best done when you are with the salesperson. Try to develop an open discussion of "how things are going." The rep may open up and tell you of some matter that does not seem important to him, but that you recognize at once deserves immediate attention. It is your greater experience that enables you to recognize when some situation is potentially explosive. The trick is to detect that there is a problem, to ferret it out, and to deal with it right away. Never allow it to fester.

Another factor may operate to destroy the effectiveness of the field contact. The sales rep may want you to scratch all your carefully made plans and rush with him to an important account to close a large pending order or to resolve some serious complaint. Should you comply? Under some circumstances you may decide that you should scrap your plans and do what the sales rep urges. On the other hand, you must recognize that this contact is one of a series in the development of the rep and that scrapping the plans will break the continuity of the development work, with possibly harmful results. Often field contacts are made infrequently; and when they are made, it is important to do those things which do the most to advance the sales rep's growth and help to achieve company objectives.

There is another aspect of this problem, and it concerns the sales rep's estimate of his own capabilities. Does he feel unprepared to close big sales or to deal with serious customer dissatisfaction? Isn't the performance of these functions part of *his* job? Would you prefer that important accounts look to you rather than to your sales rep when they have a large order to place or a complaint to adjust? If your job is to develop your sales force—and that is exactly what it is—then shouldn't you require the sales rep to think through the problem with your help until he feels that he can handle it adequately himself?

Given this problem, how are you to solve it? The best procedure is to take the time to sit down with the sales rep and talk it over thoroughly. If there is a large order to be closed, ask him why he feels unable to close it himself. What obstacles, real or imagined, are limiting him? As he talks about the account and the business to be closed, help him with the answers to those questions that bother him. Provide him with the know-how to handle the account and close the business, thus building his self-confidence. When this has been done as thoroughly as possible, finish up with a statement along these lines:

> Jo, I want you to know that the company and I want that business just as badly as you do. At the same time, you should know that I have implicit confidence in you and in your ability to get this business on your own. I am willing to risk the business by placing it in your hands because I believe it will be a minimal risk and that, with all the facts in hand, you can do as well as I can. If, on the other hand, you lack the confidence in yourself that I have in you, then I will go with you. I hope, however, that you will decide to go by yourself.

This is an important step for you to take; it is critical to your own development and growth as a sales manager, as well as to the sales rep's growth. Experience indicates that in the large majority of cases where this procedure is followed, the sales rep does decide to go by himself and actually closes the sale. The rep gains appreciably in self-confidence, which affects his future performance favorably. His customer comes to rely upon him personally. And you as sales manager have shown yourself capable of performing one of the most important functions of a manager—a willingness to take risks by delegating responsibility, thus developing those under you while increasing their motivation and capabilities.

You should review with the sales rep the order in which you have planned the performance of the various steps to be taken during the contact. Agreement must be reached on this so that the sales rep understands the relative importance of the various things to be done and the priorities that must therefore be assigned. In addition, you should make clear that two sorts of interviews will be conducted during the day: first, interviews for the purpose of making a sale or advancing the procurement of an order; and, second, interviews for the purpose of developing the sales rep and helping him toward the attainment of his agreed-upon objectives. In the former, both you and the sales rep will actively participate in the interview, whereas in the latter the sales rep will carry the ball while you merely function as an observer. Before each call, you should inform the rep as to which type of interview it will be so that he will understand your probable degree of involvement in the conduct of the interview.

It is the second kind of interview that deserves more attention. This is the interview that permits you to *observe the rep in action.* It is here that you will learn most about your sales rep and discover what you must do to help him. No reports or remarks by the sales rep concerning his problems can compare in value to what you can learn from observing such an interview. You will never know how well or how poorly your sales rep closes an order unless you permit him to conduct an interview through to the point of closing in your presence. This is not easy for a field sales manager who is champing at the bit, longing to get into the interview to "save it." Nevertheless, you must remain silent and observe. In this sort of interview, development of the sales rep is paramount and obtaining an order is of only secondary importance. The sales rep does not learn half so much by observing you in action as he learns by doing the job himself. One of the great benefits from this procedure is that the rep will become aware of his errors and weaknesses without having to have them pointed out to him. Thus it spares him the embarrassment of hearing from his boss about his weaknesses.

In one instance a sales rep turned to his field sales manager after three unsatisfactory interviews and said: "Boss, I should be kicked around the block for doing such a poor job in planning those interviews." The boss simply replied: "I'm glad you know it. Now let's see if I can help you do a better job of planning." The field sales manager, in short, will do far better when his salespeople recognize and acknowledge their own weaknesses. You will note my emphasis on the planning of the interview. Too often this aspect of a salesperson's work is not developed sufficiently. The sales manager spends most of his time with the rep in making calls. But it is the planning of those calls that is most important. The field sales manager in working with his people should give the highest priority to perfecting the planning of the interview. If this is done well, then the interview itself will be greatly improved and more effective. Don't be in a hurry to make the call when with a sales rep. Spend all the time necessary to satisfy yourself that there is a good plan.

Let's do some hypothetical observing.

As sales manager, you accompany a sales rep on the first call she has planned. This is an interview for the purpose of helping the rep with one of her agreed-upon objectives, selling product line B. You are about to drive with her to the account.

Although the chief purpose of the call is clearly understood, there is no reason why you can't learn a great deal more about the sales rep than her ability to sell product line B. The call will also provide an opportunity to improve her skill in conducting an interview; in fact, each call made by the sales rep with her manager may be of value to her overall development if you are alert to all the opportunities.

For example, while driving with her, you talk informally about the upcoming call. You ask her to bring you up to date on the account, what business the company has done with it, and the prospects for obtaining additional business. You inquire into the obstacles the company faces in trying to supply a greater share of the customer's total requirements than it does now. You want to know whether the sales rep personally knows the key decision-making people in the firm and why she feels that they should purchase product line B. You question her as to the advantages that will accrue to them through using it and how she proposes to introduce the product. You ask what sales tools she will use and in what manner.

This informal discussion will reveal the kind of planning the sales rep has done for this call. If her planning is repeatedly poor, as field sales manager you must help her improve it.

After such a discussion, which incidentally must not be an inquisition, the sales rep, upon arriving at the prospect's place of business, frequently says to her manager: "Boss, since talking with you on the way out here, I can see that I'm not really properly prepared to make this call effectively. Do you mind if we pass it up and go on to the next one?" The answer should be:

> Certainly, pass up the call. It's better not to make it at all than to do it poorly and with insufficient preparation. Let's move along. Whom do we call on next? Give me a rundown on this next account.

The process is repeated until the sales rep realizes that she has not been planning properly, and admits it. This conveniently sets the stage for you to spend time teaching her how to plan a call properly. This may be called the discussion method for helping the sales rep to improve interview planning.

Now let's suppose that you and the sales rep actually enter the prospect's place of business. You have told the sales rep to introduce you not by your title but simply as a man from the factory. You have also instructed her to pay no further attention to you but to proceed with the interview just as she would in your absence. You should then find a position that keeps you out of the limelight of the interview but that permits you to hear everything that is said.

The field sales manager knows that 75 percent of the success of an interview will depend on the nature and thoroughness of the planning done, and that the remaining 25 percent is determined by how well the sales rep executes these plans. Once the premises have been entered, the field sales manager must be alert to every situation, beginning with the approach to the receptionist.

Why the receptionist? Because many sales reps never get past the receptionist or, if they do, their approach leads to their being sent to some person who has no authority to act. For example, if the sales rep simply tells the receptionist his name and company and adds that he *sells* product line B, he may end up talking to an assistant purchasing agent instead of to the engineering staff or laboratory and production people who can requisition the product for test or purchase. The field sales manager can instruct the sales rep in the proper approach to the receptionist and even suggest key words to guide the receptionist's thinking and handling of the request for an interview. There is a great difference, for instance, between asking a receptionist: "Who is the person who *buys* products like product line B?" and inquiring: "Who is the individual *responsible* for the replacement of shaping and forming machinery?" Each question may easily result in the sales rep's being sent to a different person. Should the salesperson find that the receptionist is being made an intermediary to relay the buyer's questions, he can ask to talk directly with the buyer on the telephone. Here is an example. The salesperson picks up the phone and says:

> Mr. Smith, we saved Ajax Manufacturing a nice bit of money in their plating department, which I believe is similar to yours. I brought with me some material that will enable me to show you what we did faster than I can tell you about it over the phone. May I come up to your office so that you can see it and determine whether it is applicable to your operations?

As we have seen, the field sales manager starts his work with the salesperson long before the call is actually made. But what can he do once the actual interview has begun? Consider a situation where you and the sales rep have agreed that the rep is to conduct the interview under your observation. If you must avoid taking the interview out of the sales rep's hands, even though failure is imminent, what *is* your part in the interview? Seated some distance from the prospect and the sales rep, you listen to everything they say. Since the purpose of the call is to help the sales rep improve his skills in selling product line B, you have in your bag all the various sales tools provided by the company for presenting product line B favorably. In such a situation you may properly inject yourself into the interview at critical moments and then withdraw, letting the sales rep continue. You do this by directing your remarks to the sales rep and not to the prospect.

For instance, you may note that the interview is drooping because the salesperson is not making clear a key point that could be illustrated by a company-supplied mock-up. You take the mock-up from your bag and say to the sales rep:

> Jim, pardon me for sticking my nose into your conversation with Mr. Smith, but I could not help hearing what has been said and I wonder if Mr. Smith would be interested in seeing this mock-up. It should help answer some of the questions he is raising.

You hand the mock-up to the sales rep and then back off and resume your position at a distance. The sales rep takes the mock-up and uses it immediately.

This method of "entering and withdrawing" has been found to be extremely helpful for training purposes. Note that the sales rep is using the ideas, samples, or engineering data that the manager has handed him. *He* is finding out that *his* interviews are more effective when he uses such aids. After the interview, the manager can point out to the sales rep the value of the ideas and devices he has caused to be injected into the interview. A sales rep is ordinarily quite receptive to ideas introduced in this way and does not forget them.

The question has often been raised as to how this method can be employed when the customer knows the field sales manager well and directs his questions to him rather than to the sales rep. The answer is that the field sales manager can handle such a situation by simply referring the questions to the salesperson. For example, assume that you are greeted enthusiastically by the customer as an old friend: "Hi, Bill. How are you? I haven't seen you since you got into the big time with your company as a field sales manager.

Come in and sit down." After a reasonable amount of "horsing around," you say to the customer:

> Jim has just told me about some ideas that I think may be helpful to you. Jim, tell Mr. Smith what you had in mind.

The sales rep takes over the interview and proceeds. But the customer turns to you and asks, "Bill, what is the price of this?" You then fumble through your pocket and answer:

> I guess I've gotten a little careless since I stopped doing direct selling. I don't recall the price, but Jim here has the figures.

In short, you toss the ball right back to the sales rep every time a question is asked you by the customer. In this way, the sales rep is built up in the mind of the account, and the interview proceeds with the rep in charge and you just observing.

There is one other way for improving the quality of the interview. Have you ever noticed that when you are about to conduct an important interview, whether with your customer, boss, or some other person, you subconsciously prepare for it by subjecting yourself to a battery of questions that you *force* yourself to answer? Scores of questions pass through your mind, and you try to find convincing answers to them. After this exercise, you enter your meeting well prepared to meet almost any contingency. Because such a self-examination, which may occur while eating, dressing, or driving, is valuable preparation for an interview, why not use it deliberately as a formal part of the planning for the meeting?

With this in mind, I suggest that you prepare a list of pertinent questions to be used by salespeople in planning their interviews. This list will vary with each type of sales job. Figure 3-3 contains a typical list, and the planning and analysis sheets used by the 3M Corporation show how questions are applied in practice. The sales reps make themselves answer these questions in preparing for important interviews. With continued use, this sort of self-questioning becomes so habitual that the reps no longer require a written list.

One of your more important functions as a field sales manager is to show your salespeople the importance of relating each interview with an account to the previous and succeeding interview. In the development of an account there must be a continuity to the interviews. Each should build on the previous one, improving the position of the sales rep and of the company with the account. How can you teach this concept most effectively to the sales rep? Here is one time-tested method.

(text continues on page 52)

Figure 3-3. Questions intended to improve a sales rep's preparedness when planning an interview.

1. Is this actually a key account? Is it worth the time and effort? Why?
2. Should this call have priority over other calls to be made today? Why?
3. Should a phone call for an appointment be made? Do I want to meet with more than one individual and how can I achieve this?
4. When was my last call?
5. What happened? Why? What am I going to do about it?
6. Whom do I plan to see? Is this the right person? If not, what can I do about it?
7. Who can decide to change the source of supply? Who is the decision-making authority?
8. How can I reach this person without antagonizing others?
9. Where does the company buy now? Why? What percentage, if any, of its needs do we supply? Is this satisfactory? If not, what do I propose to do about it?
10. Is there really any good reason why this company should buy from us?
11. Are there any specific sales tools, samples, letters, or proposals that I should use? Do I have them on hand? When and how should I introduce them?
12. Do I want to visit the plant or warehouse? How will I do this? What obstacles are likely to arise, and how can I overcome them?
13. What will I do when I do get out to the plant or warehouse?
14. Is the purpose of this call to secure an order? What order? Is this goal realistic?
15. If not to secure an order, what is the purpose of this call?
16. Is my purpose a sound one?
17. If the customer is dissatisfied for any reason, how will I handle the situation?
18. Is this call an important step in the overall development of the account? How? If not, why not?
19. What other obstacles are likely to arise, and how will I meet them?
20. What can I do on this call, in addition to making a sale, that will lay the groundwork for another sale on my next call or in the near future? How? With whom? With what sales tools, aids, or samples?

(continues)

Figure 3-3. (cont.)

Pre-Call Planning Sheet

PRE-APPROACH　Form 30431

The best feeling you can have going into a game is that of honest, thorough preparation.
John Madden

Total Potential/Year $ _____

3M Now $ _____　Competition $ _____

Name of Account　　　　　　　　Type of Business

Rating AA · A · B · C

Calls budgeted per year _____

If account was not sold on previous call, what was the reason and what can I do to get the order on this call?	Competitive Products, System, Services in Use. Prices

Needs, wants, goals of the Account. What problems or conditions can we eliminate or improve?	Solutions

Objectives/results to be achieved on this call	Whom do I want to contact, title, why?
1.	1.
2.	2.
3.	3.
4.	4.

Exhibits, Samples, Sales Aids to be used

Attention

Involvement

Questions to ask

Understanding – Agreement

Product, Service, System, Company, Idea, Yourself

Feature	Advantage	Problem	Benefit Explains the value to the buyer and answers the want, can be separated into two parts		Evidence
Describes what it is (or) what are its parts, usually the opposite of the solution	Explains what the features do (or) describes the function of the features, usually the opposite of the problem	Explain the problem the advantage solves or explains what is preventing the fulfillment of needs and wants, usually the opposite of the advantage	Company Benefit Save/make money Save time/better use of time Make job easier/products better Save lives/improve health	Personal benefit Recognition Achievement Security Personal profit or pleasure	Proof to be used 3rd party models Exhibit Demonstration
Noun	Adjective, verb or adverb				
Because of	You can	And avoid	Which means		

Objections　If any　　　　　　　　Logical Answers

Action　What commitment do I want to achieve?　　　　What is my next step?　　Date?

POST-CALL ANALYSIS

Visualization of the successful outcome of the call, before you make it, increases your success ratio

On a scale of one to ten how effective was the sales call?　Why?

Form 30431

(continues)

Figure 3–3. (cont.)

Post-Call Analysis Sheet

PRE-APPROACH   Form 30430

The best feeling you can have going into a game is that of honest, thorough preparation.
John Madden

Name of Account _____ Type of Business _____

Total Potential/Year $ _____

3M Now $ _____ Competition $ _____

Rating AA - A - B - C

Calls budgeted per year _____

If account was not sold on previous call, what was the reason and what can I do to get the order on this call?

- What additional information was obtained to add to change your original analysis?

Competitive Products, System, Services in Use, Prices
- Was your competitive analysis correct? If not, what additional competitive information would you like to have?
- Where and how many would you gain this information?
- Was assessment of the total potential of the account correct?

Needs, wants, goals of the Account. What problems or conditions can we eliminate or improve?

- Was your analysis of needs - wants - goals - problems correct?
- What changes would you make in your original analysis?
- Did you uncover or make prospect/customer aware of real problems?

Solutions
- Why was your solution correct? If not,
- What changes or additions would you make in the solutions presented?

Objectives/results to be achieved on this call
1. Was objective achieved? If not,
2. What should be my next objective?
3.
4.

Whom do I want to contact, title, why?
1. How do you know you are calling on right buying influence?
2. Who else should be targeted for future calls?
3. How would you describe the motivational profile of your customer?
4. How can you use this for future calls?

Exhibits, Samples, Sales Aids to be used:
- What additional materials would have proven beneficial?

Attention
- What technique was used?
- Was it received favorably?

Involvement

Questions to ask
- Was a benefit claim used?
- What needs - wants - goals - problems were uncovered, identified, expressed?
- Did I make a conscious attempt to listen to the prospect?

Form 30430

Understanding – Agreement

Product, Service, System, Company, Idea, Yourself

Feature	Advantage	Problem	Benefit	Evidence
Describes what it is (or) what are its parts, usually the opposite of the solution	Explains what the features do (or) describes the function of the features, usually the opposite of the problem	Explain the problem the advantage solves or explains what is preventing the fulfillment of needs and wants, usually the opposite of the advantage	Explains the value to the buyer and answers the want, can be seperated into two parts	Proof to be used 3rd party incident Exhibit Demonstration
Noun	Adjective, verb or adverb		Company Benefit / Save/make money / Save time/better use of time / Make job easier/products better / Save lives/improve health — Personal benefit / Recognition / Achievement / Security / Personal profit or pleasure	
Because of	You can	And avoid	Which means	

- What advantages and benefits were used to match up with the needs - wants - goals - problems of the account?
- How did the customer/prospect indicate the benefits presented would match up and satisfy the needs - wants - goals - problems of the account?
- What caused you to feel the evidence you used was believed and understood by the account?
- Was checking question used to pin down Agreement at end of each FAB?

Objections   If any
- What objections were raised that could have been overcome before they came up.

Logical Answers
- How and where will I get the answers to the objections I couldn't answer effectively?

- What will I do on the next call to accomplish this?
- How can I improve the techniques I used to overcome objections?

Action
What commitment do I want to achieve?
- Which close was used?   - What action was asked for?
- Were buying signals recognized, could close have come sooner?

What is my next step?   Date?
- Is objective firmed up for next call?   - Buying influences involved?
- Appointments made, what commitments did I make?

POST-CALL ANALYSIS

On a scale of one to ten, how effective was the sales call? Why?

Reprinted with permission from the 3M Corporation, St. Paul, Minnesota.

The best time to plan for the next interview is at the moment the sales rep leaves the premises of the customer. At that moment he vividly recalls every detail of the interview. He remembers his achievements and failings and knows what he must do next to further develop the account and advance the position of his company and himself. He also knows when the next call should be made. He can enter this date in his diary so that it will not be forgotten. He can take a moment to make notes on his customer sheet or card indicating the next step to be taken. Doing this after each interview is in reality performance of vital steps 3 and 4 of the cycle of management (in Figure 1-1). The best way for you to teach this procedure is to make sure that the sales rep follows it after every call on which you have accompanied him. You can also look over the records of each sales rep to see whether they are making similar notations after solo calls.

There are a number of other skills you may find it necessary to teach your salespeople while you are with them in the field. One of these involves the method of concluding a field contact. The field contact, when conducted in the manner I have just described, will disclose certain strengths and weaknesses of the sales rep. It is important that there be agreement between you and each sales rep with respect to both qualities. A discussion of these strengths and weaknesses should be the basis on which you plan your next field contact with the sales rep, suggesting guidelines for areas where performance should be improved by the time you return for another field contact. These objectives for the development of the rep should be clearly determined before you leave and should be promptly confirmed in writing. When the next field contact is planned, these objectives will be the principal basis for such planning. Thus continuity of the program for the development of the sales rep is achieved.

Among the many aspects of the sales rep's performance in the field that you should observe and, where necessary, correct are the following:

- The extent to which the sales rep employs the telephone to save time, increase effectiveness, and improve performance
- How the sales rep covers the territory in order to be where the business is when it is going to be placed
- The amount of time the sales rep spends on keeping various records
- The way the rep handles customers' complaints
- The attitude of the salesperson toward headquarters and its policies
- The rep's general attitude toward work and life

As manager, you must always be alert to the sales rep in relation to these factors and be prepared to step in and correct any weaknesses as they become apparent. It is during field contact that you can deal with these problems most successfully. They are not likely to be remedied by letters or even telephone calls to the sales rep from the branch office. Let's therefore consider some of the methods that have worked best in dealing with them.

The most successful salespeople are those who make the maximum use of the telephone. One field sales manager has said that when he arrives at an airport to visit his star salesman he always knows where to find him—in a telephone booth. Even at noon, when the two go to lunch, he will tell the manager what to order for him and then make a phone call while waiting to be served. There is nothing unusual about such conduct. There are sales reps who understand the value of their time and are unwilling to waste any of it. Their success is generally predictable.

One trap in the path of sales reps who try to use their time to best advantage is the emergency message telling them to drop everything and run to a customer who demands to see them at once. It they listen to this siren song, all their good planning goes out the window. Top-notch salespeople have an excellent way of handling these SOSs and can usually take care of the needs of their customers without disrupting their own plans. How do they do it? With the telephone. When sales reps who use their time expertly return to their office or home at the end of a day's work, they usually find a list of phone calls requiring attention. If their territory is out of town, they may phone in every evening for such messages. Upon receipt of the messages they immediately classify them as follows:

- Those from customers they can call back the same night and perhaps catch at home
- Those from customers they can call very early the next morning
- Those customers they will call while making their rounds the next day

Thus all get attention without interfering with the rep's planned program.

Aggressive salespeople use the phone while they are waiting to see a customer, while traveling between interviews, while waiting to be served in restaurants, and while waiting for their cars to be serviced. They do not waste time at home or in the office returning the previous day's phone calls; they do this from the field. They never make a visit as a result of a phone call before first returning that phone call. Frequently, a phone call is merely a request for information that can be given as easily over the phone as through a personal visit. Phone calls are also used to make certain that the prospect is available and will receive the sales rep. When returning phone calls, salespeople should have their diaries in front of them so that they can make a definite appointment to see the customer if this appears necessary. Very often the customer will not insist that the sales rep "drop everything" and come right over but will be satisfied to make an appointment at a time that will not disrupt the rep's plans. The sales rep should not hesitate to *ask* for a convenient appointment while also indicating a willingness to "drop everything" if necessary.

The telephone is also useful in making sure that customers located out of the city are at their place of business when the sales rep proposes to call. Where it is desirable for the sales rep to meet with more than one person at the customer's office or plant, this kind of meeting can be arranged in advance through the use of the telephone. Telephone calls cost much less than personal calls. Wherever a telephone call can substitute for a personal call, it is more economical and usually just as effective. The telephone frees salespeople to put their time to the best use so that they can be where the business is when it is going to be placed.

An important use of the telephone is to set up an appointment with an account on short notice. Occasionally, the sales rep finds himself in the neighborhood of an account that he had not planned to call upon that day. Unexpectedly finding that he has time to make the call, he telephones from the place of his last call to find out whether this customer will see him. By making the phone call here, the sales rep is saving time. If the customer is unavailable, then the sales rep can perhaps phone still another account and thus get in an additional call during the day.

Such phone calls must be as carefully planned as an interview. They are actually interviews conducted over the telephone in preparation for a more lengthy, personal interview. It is easy for the customer or prospect at the other end of the line to be curt or to refuse to see the sales rep. Experience indicates that the best psychological approach under such circumstances is for sales reps to identify themselves with some important account or person in the industry, remarking, for example:

Hello, Mr. Smith. I am just leaving the office of Mr. Weath-

erby, chief engineer at General Electric, and am about fifteen
minutes away from your office. If you'll be in for the next
fifteen minutes, I'll be right over. Will you be there? O.K. I'm
starting now. Goodbye.

The sales rep has asked a direct question; as soon as he receives an
affirmative reply, he hangs up and is on his way.

In another situation the sales rep is asking for an interview over
the phone but does not have a close relationship with the person to
whom he is talking. He again plans an approach likely to interest
the customer:

> Hello, Mr. Smith. This is Bill Jones of Acme Manufacturing.
> We have just completed some work at General Electric that
> resulted in considerable savings in their plant operations in a
> situation very similar to what you probably have in your widget
> division. I'm at Smith Company now and have the data with
> me, and if you'll be there for fifteen minutes, I can come right
> over to see you. Will you be there? O.K. I'll be there.

He hangs up and gets going.

The preceding examples illustrate the kind of telephone interviews that can be effective. A major problem in this kind of interview arises when the customer asks the sales rep, in effect, to give
the entire interview over the telephone. Experience indicates that
the sales rep should refuse with some such statement as:

> I can show you more quickly than I can tell you. If you'll be
> there for fifteen minutes, I'll bring in some material that will
> quickly give you the information you want. O.K.?

Many an interview is lost because the sales rep is required to
talk to the customer from the lobby by telephone. This possibility
should be anticipated by the sales rep, and the sales presentation for
such a situation should be carefully planned. Few receptionists are
prepared for sales reps who have carefully thought through the "interview with the receptionist." Most reps, however, never realize
the importance of *getting* through *the receptionist* to the decision-making
authority. If you were to sit in the lobby of a large concern you
would observe that sales reps in general follow the same routine.
They enter, place their cards before the receptionist, wait to be
guided to anyone this person feels is proper, and are prepared to sit
around for a considerable time until this happens.

Top-performing salespeople, on the other hand, show some interesting variations from this procedure. They usually know the best time to call on an account and, if it is necessary to make the call very early in the morning in order to be first in line, they plan their day accordingly. In some cases they may even arrive before the receptionist reports for work in the morning.

Upon presenting herself, the top sales rep rarely uses her business card. She provides information as it is requested of her—but no more than requested. If the receptionist asks for her card, she replies that she has none. When asked her name, she answers: "Brown." When asked the name of her company, she answers "Acme." When asked exactly what it is she wants to talk about, she requests the receptionist's permission to use the phone so that she can speak directly with the prospect. If this is given, the sales rep states concisely what she wants to talk about, what kind of problems she can solve for the customer, and where she has helped to solve similar problems. She asks leave to show what she has brought with her, saying that she can demonstrate faster than she can explain and suggesting that the customer either come down to the lobby or invite her to his office. Such a well-planned phone interview very often leads to a profitable face-to-face interview with the customer. The telephone has proved an effective tool because its use has been carefully planned.

Field observation by the sales manager of the manner in which salespeople use or misuse the telephone can determine the amount and kind of instruction to be given each sales rep in this connection.

Another important area to be observed by the field sales manager on a field trip is the kind and quality of territorial coverage given by the sales rep. *Territorial coverage means being where the business is when it is going to be placed.* It varies greatly with the particular field of selling. For instance, in calling upon consumers it may be preferable for the sales rep to follow a regular route. In the soft-goods business, by contrast, salespeople must be quite selective as to how they will cover the territory. When sales reps go on the road with a new line, they usually want to call upon all the larger accounts as quickly as possible before the competition can get to them. They cannot afford the time to call on most of the smaller accounts but must reach them on a follow-up trip after their first swing through the territory. Even where the company provides a list of accounts to be called on weekly, sales reps may at their own discretion depart from this list when they feel justified in doing so. In the case of industrial sales reps, the decision as to when to make a call is left largely with the individual.

In my discussion of the planning session, I suggested that the manager ask the sales rep to determine when he proposed to put his account-development strategy into effect, and then to enter the name of the account in his or her (the rep's) diary under the date decided on. In this way every important account is listed in the diary under a date that indicates when the first call is to be made to carry out the strategy or plan for the development of that account during the year ahead. The sales rep must keep the name of that account dated ahead in his diary for his next call.

This diary notation, as I have mentioned, is best made immediately after each call. In selecting the date, the sales rep will consider the approximate date when the account should be seen again and the date nearest to that time when his diary calls for him to be in the same zone. In this way the name of the account comes up automatically for call on the optimum date for making that call. In many cases the sales rep carries his diary with him, and at the conclusion of the call says to the customer:

> I'll bring the proposal in to you as soon as the engineering department completes the drawing. This will be in about three weeks. Suppose I get back here with it about the 25th of the month. How does that strike you? Is 10 A.M. on the 25th convenient for you? Well, then, will you please note it on your calendar? I'll put it in my diary.

Thus the sales rep sets up an appointment for his return call and saves considerable time. If he feels any uncertainty about the customer's keeping the appointment, he may phone or write a few days in advance to confirm the appointment or, if necessary, change it to a more convenient time for the customer. If the appointment is rescheduled, the sales rep notes it in his diary.

The number of calls made on an account will vary greatly with the activity of the account, the time of year, and other circumstances. The important factor is that these calls not be made mechanically in accordance with some preconceived formula but instead take place on dates based on the sales rep's appraisal of the need to revisit the account. This method develops the sales rep because it makes him responsible for servicing the account. He feels that he is really in charge of his territory and responsible for the development of the accounts in it.

The degree to which a sales rep performs this function lends itself readily to supervision. As manager, you can observe it during a field contact, and can instruct or correct as you think necessary. At the same time you can notice whether the sales rep's time is being spent advantageously in other respects. For example, when the sales rep leaves an important account at three in the afternoon, has she planned to use the remaining time calling upon two or three smaller accounts in the vicinity? Does the sales rep spend too much time with small accounts to the neglect of some of the more important ones? Does the sales rep use her time well in the interview? If there are a number of individuals to be seen at a single account, does she try to see as many as possible on the same call? Does she present her story so thoroughly and competently that a single call accomplishes as much as two or three calls made by a poorer sales person? Does she drive long distances out of her way to see people from whom she can expect little of value? Does she pass up valuable business because she habitually fails to call on certain inconveniently located accounts? Does she waste valuable time by unnecessarily retracing her steps while working her territory? Although these questions may seem obvious, they should be asked. One field sales manager, working with a rep in a town where a bridge over a river marked the central area, noted that the sales rep crossed that bridge seven times during the day.

It is an important function of sales management to improve the sales rep's use of time. This can be done most effectively in the field. As field sales manager you have an opportunity to observe the attitudes of sales reps toward their job, their company, their customers, and the instruction you are giving them. If you are skilled in maintaining a relaxed, informal manner, the sales reps are likely to "let down their hair" with respect to their feelings and attitudes. Their handling of a customer complaint or other problem, their reaction to some company policy or procedure, their acceptance of instruction, their remarks about family and living conditions will all indicate either that you have a very promising, sound sales rep to develop—or that there are dangerous undercurrents that may affect a particular sales rep's growth, performance, or even tenure with the company. As manager you can tactfully bring such matters to the surface and deal with them through counseling with the sales rep.

For example, the sales rep may complain about the amount of time he must spend making out reports and doing other paperwork. He may say, "I spend about three hours every night at my desk. When do I have a chance to be with my wife and kids, to take in a movie, or to be with friends?'' You may then spend the evening with the sales rep, showing him how to do his paperwork more quickly; or, as in one case, you can demonstrate how to get most of it done during the day as the rep makes his calls. With the cause of his dissatisfaction gone, the attitude of the sales rep should improve greatly. And only in the field can a manager take such action.

The question is often raised as to the extent to which a field sales manager should become involved in dealing with the personal habits or problems of the sales force: whether they drink to excess, whether their home lives are happy, whether they are unfaithful to their spouses, or whether they have financial problems. In general, you should be guided by the extent to which these problems or habits affect the image of the company or the sales rep's effectiveness and productivity. You are not a social worker and should not attempt to reform your sales staff. It need be no concern of yours if the sales rep has faults of a personal nature or personal problems so long as they do not adversely affect the sales rep's performance as a company employee. When a habit or problem does impair the image of the company and the relationship of the company with its prospects and customers, or when it stands in the way of the sales rep's ability to absorb training and to develop, then you must promptly take steps to correct the situation.

On occasion, a sales rep may voluntarily bring some personal problem to you and ask your help in solving it. In such a situation you should welcome the opportunity to be helpful to the sales rep and thus cement your relationship. A highly motivated, top-notch sales rep may be overextended financially or may be having some problem with a family member—for example, a daughter's dissatisfaction with the city in which they are living. Your advice and help as manager may be an important factor in resolving the problem.

The field sales manager is management, and the field contact is best calculated to get this idea across to the sales force. The manager is not a member of the sales rep's group but is the direct representative of the top executives of the company, the interpreter of their thinking and their policies. It is through the manager that salespeople and their families receive their impression of the company. Just how can the field sales manager promote the acceptance of this concept? Certainly not by proclaiming that he or she is the boss or by arbitrarily laying down the law and demanding strict compliance with such dictates. The business world has no place for the person who attempts to whip people into obedience and conformity.

As field sales manager you will win the confidence and respect of your salespeople only after you have made them realize that you want to help them and that you actually have helped them to grow and develop. It has been said that the most accurate appraisal of the effectiveness of a field sales manager is one that he never hears. It is made by the sales rep after they have parted at the end of a field contact. The sales rep either says, "Thank God he is gone and I can get back to doing my job," or, "I wish he would come down here more often. I really learned a great deal today. That guy sure is helpful."

A good manager must be willing to take the risks involved in giving salespeople the greatest responsibility compatible with what they can discharge effectively. Instead of breathing down their necks and supervising every step each sales rep takes, you must give them a chance to perform on their own with little or no supervision and see how well they do. You should delegate responsibility but not lose control of the reps, giving them specific jobs to do, objectives to be achieved. You must make sure they do the job, but in their own way without interference. After assessing how well a rep is doing, you may help that individual to do the job better. The sales rep's response will be amazing in most instances. People given responsibility usually rise to the occasion. As field sales manager you can do much to win your men and women to your side by letting them know that you have confidence in them and proving it.

Planning is particularly important; you should plan with your reps. Having helped to develop the plans, they will then assume a greater share of the responsibility for carrying them out.

It is important that you understand your people and recognize any obstacles that may be blocking their complete acceptance of your leadership. For example, a veteran sales rep may resent a young field sales manager. You must win him over—to start with, by showing respect for his age and years of service. You may tell him:

> I had little to do with my assignment to my present post. But, now that I have the job, I want to do it well. Perhaps you could do the job even better, but that is not what management wanted. My success depends upon how helpful I can be to you and the other reps. I want a chance to work with you, to profit from your great experience, and perhaps to bring you some ideas that will help you to do even better and to derive more satisfaction from your job.

Then, if the older man still will not fall into line, you may have to exercise your authority and be somewhat tougher.

Similarly, the young field sales manager may have a problem with the sales rep who was his peer just a short time ago. They often commiserated together. Now one is the other's boss. It has been a hard pill for the sales rep to swallow, and his wife also is unhappy about it. Both suffer from wounded pride. Such a situation requires understanding on the part of the field sales manager. If this is your problem, I suggest that you discuss the matter openly with the sales rep, indicating that management has made the decision, and that as the new manager you are prepared to do everything possible to succeed at your job. You should explain that this means helping the people under you to develop and become promotable. Perhaps the sales rep left behind can be the next selection of top management when another field sales manager is required.

This leads to a final word about the relationship between the manager and his team and how it can be built into something valuable. Some managers feel that their concern for the sales reps should be limited to their work. They have no interest in their domestic or social life or in any other aspect of their personal affairs unless it affects the company. Fortunately, most managers lean toward a warmer relationship with their salespeople. The so-called buddy-buddy relationship is to be abhorred, of course. The manager, in an effort to ingratiate himself with his sales reps should never join in their gripes about the company or promise to "take up" matters with the big bosses when he has no intention of doing so. We have all heard this sort of comment too many times:

> You might as well go ahead and do this because the big bosses at the home office insist upon it. I know the idea is no good and a waste of time just as well as you do, but what can we poor guys out here in the field do about it? Those big shots never listen to us.

What is just as bad is for the manager to make promises that he never intends or lacks the courage to keep. He routinely says, "I'll take it up with the main office." But he never does. The sales reps soon "get his number" and he loses all effectiveness with them. This much is certain: *The field sales manager must be the champion of his company when he is in the field with his team, and the champion of his reps when he is at the head office.* This little rule states the function of the field sales manager as a part of management when he is in the field and as a communicator of his reps' reactions to his supervisors when he meets with them. He may dine with some of the salespeople and

their spouses and enjoy a feeling of friendship and warmth with
them. Yet he must not fraternize with his reps or allow his social
relations with them to affect his performance as sales manager.

Key Accounts

The field sales manager's responsibility for key accounts varies with
the particular company. In general this responsibility is of two kinds:

1. *Direct responsibility.* The manager is personally charged with
   selling and developing important accounts within the district
   or region. No other salesperson is involved.
2. *Indirect responsibility.* One of the sales reps is directly responsible for the account.

Direct Responsibility

If you are a manager with direct responsibility, you must have
a clear understanding with your superiors as to the relative importance of your duty to sell important accounts and your responsibility
for developing sales reps. In some companies the manager is in
reality a supersales rep with primary responsibility for important
accounts. In this case you must devote the bulk of your time to these
important accounts, and you will be appraised mostly on your ability to sell and develop these accounts, while at the same time giving
some attention to the one or two people you supervise. In other
companies you will be judged primarily on your success or failure
in developing the salespeople under you, while at the same time you
are expected personally to develop a limited number of "house accounts," "national accounts," or "key accounts." In each case it
is important that you plan your time so as to accomplish what is
expected of you.

Indirect Responsibility

In this case every sales rep under you has been assigned a few
important accounts. Top management wants the business from these
accounts and would like to establish a strong, durable relationship
with them, a relationship that will not be broken if any one sales
rep leaves the company, retires, or dies. Management therefore
wants the important people in these accounts to know the manager

and to have some regular contact with him. This type of manager may also coordinate the work of various sales reps who call on different facilities of the same account or its headquarters. To accomplish this, you should proceed as follows:

1. Identify these accounts.
2. Determine exactly how your sales reps stand with each of these important accounts.
3. In planning field contacts with your salespeople, give some consideration to visiting these accounts so as to ensure that you are performing your special function of strengthening the company's and the sales rep's position with the account while simultaneously establishing your own personal relationship. Carefully planned and executed interviews by the sales rep and the manager working as a team often accomplish so much that you need visit the account with the sales rep only two or three times a year.
4. If a territory is vacant, step into the situation and hold the important accounts until a replacement is secured.
5. Use your position to help the sales rep reach the higher echelons within the account. In doing so you carry out a valuable and important function.

Where the sales rep has the primary responsibility for an account, you as manager must be careful not to permit the rep to delegate this responsibility to you. Neither should you take such responsibility away from the sales rep by making sales or settling complaints where the rep is charged with these duties.

Developing the Junior Sales Rep

Some companies have obtained excellent results by assigning new and inexperienced sales reps to work directly under a qualified senior salesperson in the assigned territory or in an adjoining territory. The idea is not always workable and requires evaluation by each company to determine its applicability. The main advantages of this training method are as follows;

1. Since she can delegate the easier tasks to the younger person, the senior sales rep will have more time to devote to matters

that require greater skill and experience; consequently, sales volume will be increased.

2. The new, less experienced sales rep will receive closer supervision than would be the case if the entire supervisory job were performed by the field sales manager. This means accelerated growth for the new sales rep and fewer trainee failures. Of course, the manager still has the primary responsibility for the development of the new salesperson. However, assigning the new rep to a qualified senior salesperson makes for a closer working relationship and helps the junior over many obstacles. At the same time, the senior also benefits because she is given an opportunity to learn the art of developing people. In short, her own qualifications for a managerial job can be evaluated.

The senior sales rep is usually prepared for this new responsibility with some special training, perhaps a week or two at headquarters and some close supervision by the field sales manager. The choice should be someone with real interest in helping others, one who accepts company policies and whose performance has been above average. This person should receive increased compensation in recognition of her taking on greater responsibility and contributing her valuable time.

The new sales rep must recognize that this kind of assignment affords a better opportunity for growth than would be the case if he were assigned cold to a new territory of his own without the intensive help of a senior sales rep. He must be made to feel that this assignment will not lessen his opportunities for growth and promotion and that eventually he too is expected to become a senior sales rep. The whole point of the training program is to make him better prepared to take on the full sales job.

This arrangement calls for a carefully studied compensation plan ensuring that both the senior and the new sales rep are fairly compensated. Where the plan contemplates the senior's defraying the entire cost of the additional sales rep out of her own compensation, the company frequently will reimburse her for the first year. Basically, the senior sales rep must benefit financially from the plan, and the new sales rep must be adequately paid. When sufficient additional business is procured, there will be no problem. But in the interim, while the new sales rep is learning the ropes, compensation may have to be absorbed by management as a training cost rather than as a charge against the actual productivity of the territory in which the rep is training.

Customer Group Meetings

If as field sales manager you can fit a few hundred dollars into your budget for meetings at which your salespeople can talk to groups of customers and prospective customers, increased sales may result. Such meetings are a very inexpensive device for building up both the sales rep's and the company's image. They are an excellent way to break into accounts that have been difficult to sell, and they also provide access to the higher, decision-making echelons of a company without offending lower-level personnel. When there is news of some new product, method, or advance in technology and you feel that the information will be of real value to customers and prospects, you may suggest a customer group meeting to acquaint them with it. Naturally, the meeting must be thoroughly planned. The first step is to find out whether headquarters will help or whether the entire burden of setting up the meeting must be borne by the district or branch office. Certainly it would be unwise to place the entire burden on the sales reps; their job is selling, not being facilitators. Therefore, you must resolve the following questions:

1. Who will contact the people to be invited?
2. Who will send them invitations and follow up to find out how many will actually attend?
3. Who will select and prepare the props—the mock-ups, slides, or films? Who will make sure that a projector and screen will be on hand?
4. Who will arrange for the meeting place and the luncheon or supper? Who will prepare and set up the room for the meeting?

Suffice it to say that as manager you must plan the details of this kind of program before you can suggest it to your sales force.

Once the stage has been set, the sales rep can be offered an opportunity to conduct customer group meetings. Experience indicates that a good meeting can be held with as few as fifteen customers and prospects, or as many as 200. The audience for industrial sales meetings of this kind usually ranges from twenty-five to fifty people. It is not my purpose to go into detail concerning procedures since these will vary from one company to another. I merely suggest such meetings as an excellent way to reach certain people who are important to you in a given territory and to enlist their interest in what you can do for them. When good, regular customers are mixed with others who have never been sold, the results are almost universally beneficial. The good customers ''sell'' the others.

The best meetings are carefully timed. Usually they are held at noon with a luncheon provided. The plan that has worked out best is to allow about one hour for the lunch itself, a half-hour for a formal presentation by the sales rep, and a half-hour for discussion and questions.

Some companies send factory personnel to speak at such meetings, and in some instances the field sales manager conducts them. The most lasting results, however, are obtained when the sales rep— the man or woman the account sees throughout the year—is the person to stand up in front of the audience and make the presentation. It has also been found that citing local uses of company products or services is very effective, especially when accompanied by photos, slides, or motion pictures.

The Top-Notch Sales Rep

The greatest asset of a sales organization is the consistently top-notch sales rep who is now or shortly will be promotable. Yet salespeople of this caliber are often neglected by their managers, who feel that since they are doing so well, they require little attention. The purpose of this discussion is to point up two important facts in this connection.

First, the top-notch sales rep must have objectives just as any other salesperson has. No sales rep ever develops the territory to its full potential. One excellent sales rep, on being complimented by his supervisor, said: ''I've just scratched the surface of my territory.'' In fact, in order to hold very good sales reps the manager must often find ways of helping them to do even better. The story is told of a sales rep who, having led his organization for several successive years, responded to his supervisor's praise as follows: ''Whatever I have achieved is due to the excellent training you have given me. I want you to know that I am not satisfied with my own performance and must do better. You tell me what I must do, and I will follow your guidance.'' Thus the manager and the sales rep should set objectives for the latter's further growth and development. The work of the sales rep should be properly supervised through field contacts, and the results should be reviewed periodically. The next steps to be taken should be agreed upon and fed back into improved planning.

Second, the manager must recognize that some of the very best sales ideas come from the field. Seldom does the manager "dream up" wonderful sales techniques and ideas while sitting at a desk. *Observing the top-notch sales rep in action is one of the most important functions of the field sales manager,* provided that he or she is alert to superior methods and techniques that can be transmitted to other salespeople. Performance manuals easily become obsolete unless they are freshened with new methods that are successfully meeting current needs. The methods that worked well for sales reps four or five years ago may not be the best methods to use today. To find the methods that are currently the most successful, the manager should observe the operations and performance of the sales reps who are consistently getting top results. Some field contacts with top people may be made solely for the purpose of observing them and nothing else.

There was once an organization whose sales were falling except in the case of three or maybe four top sales reps. The sales manager decided that it was finally time to do something. He took it upon himself to write to each rep individually, saying in essence that he wanted the chance to observe them on a most personal basis. Here is what he wrote:

> I would like to spend a couple of days with you simply observing everything you do from the time you get up in the morning until the time you go to bed at night. Plan these two days just as you would if I were not going to be with you. I want to be an observer because I may be able to learn something from you.

The manager observed the planning of each of these reps, the way they covered the territory, their method of handling the sales interview, the way in which they handled phone calls, the time they spent after working hours in preparing for the next day's work—in short, every phase of each sales rep's operation. Each night, after returning to his hotel, he wrote down the salient impressions he had formed as a result of the day's observations. And, after this close study of his four leading sales reps, he found that there were several things that each was doing. The manager particularly noted these "common" methods that were being employed and decided that, although they departed from the methods then being taught, they were more effective than those given in "the book." He then taught these new ideas to his other reps, and an immediate improvement in their sales resulted.

Sales Reps' Expenses

In some organizations the total expenses of the field sales manager are budgeted, and he has full responsibility for how this money is spent. In others the manager merely supervises or audits the expenditures of his office and his salespeople and assumes responsibility for keeping expenses in line. In still other instances sales reps, who may be paid on a commission basis, bear their expenses; any report to the company is only for tax purposes. Is there one rule that applies to all these situations? Yes. It is that field sales managers have the responsibility for teaching their staffs how to perform their functions at the lowest possible cost commensurate with effective operations. It is a matter not of who pays but rather of how efficiently the salesperson operates. The manager is primarily interested in performance, and good performance by a sales rep seldom goes hand in hand with high expenses. Where a sales rep's expenses appear excessive, the manager must determine the reason and then get that rep to agree to a course of action that will reduce them. The same rule applies to office expenses.

The story is told of the young sales rep who was about to go on the road for the first time. He went to his father, an old-time star salesman, and asked for his advice on expenses. The father replied, "If your expenses are five cents a week and you fail to sell anything, they are too high."

In some cases effective sales management is weakened because the manager places too much emphasis on every expense item the sales rep reports. Rather, managers should be concerned with helping their salespeople achieve their agreed-upon objectives, and they should obtain their participation and cooperation in the achievement of this goal. But excessive expenses over an extended period are an indication that a sales rep is not working as efficiently as he or she should, is not performing at full capacity, or is immature and using very poor judgment. In the latter instance, one might further suspect that poor judgment is also affecting other areas of the sales rep's work. In any event it is the manager's function to get at the root of the matter and correct it.

On the other hand, expenses beyond the norm may be incurred for very good reasons. A sales rep who covers a very large geographical area is apt to incur much greater expenses than others with more compact territories. In some instances companies have provided extra compensation for such salespeople to place them on an equal footing with sales reps in territories of normal size. There are also

many instances where companies, recognizing that entertainment is a part of the sales job in their particular business, provide all or part of the necessary funds. These special examples show how important it is for the field sales manager to sit down with his reps and analyze their sales expenses in a constructive way.

The essential thing is for the manager and each sales rep to agree upon the amount of expense that can be considered proper and, therefore, justified.

4

The Appraisal Process

Efficient appraisal by the field sales manager consists of the following:

1. Regular evaluation of the progress made by each of your sales reps toward agreed-upon objectives
2. Regular evaluation of your own progress toward such objectives
3. Recognition of what must be done, an understanding of how to do it, and the allocation of time for that purpose

Review! Review! Review! "How Are We Doing?"

To place appraisal in proper perspective, so that you fully recognize its importance in the management job, it should be recalled that *appraisal is the third step in the cycle of management.* After you have been coaching your sales reps, supervising their work, instructing them, and showing them how to do the job better, you pause and take a long look to determine whether progress is being made. Although appraisal is a continuous process, periodically it is formalized by preparing a written summary of all that has happened and then deciding on a course of action. This is followed by coaching—a discussion of the appraisal with the sales rep. Actually, any discussion of a sales rep's performance you have with him or her is a form of coaching. It may just be a pat on the back, an offhand compliment, or perhaps an effort to correct a weakness. Coaching will be effective provided that the sales rep recognizes and accepts it as a means of help.

Appraisal cannot take place in a vacuum. It is a form of measurement. When the linesman in a football game measures distance to determine whether a team has a first down, he is appraising that team's ability to move the ball forward by ten yards. The ten-yard standard is set by the rules of the game and is the measure against which a valid appraisal may be made. Similarly, a valid appraisal of a sales rep's performance must be made against some agreed-upon measure. Three significant criteria for the appraisal of a sales rep are:

1. *The description of the sales rep's job.* The rep agreed to this description in accepting the job. (If you do not have such a description of the job for your reps, you need not await action by your boss but can prepare one yourself or, better yet, ask your sales reps to write down their understanding of the job.)

2. *What, specifically, is expected of the sales rep?* In other words, What are the standards of performance? This list includes figures such as the expected dollar volume or the number of units sold in a given period, the number of new accounts opened, the maximum amount of money allowed for expenses, and any other specific and/or measurable requirements of the job.

3. *The objectives for the rep's development and growth.* These are the goals that you and the sales rep agreed upon at the planning session previously discussed in Chapter 2 ("Planning: The First Step").

Sales reps who are aware of these measures are anxious to learn how they are doing. They want the manager's appraisal of their performance. Skillful appraisal and coaching can definitely improve a sales rep's attitude and sales. They can keep him or her on the right track and speed up that individual's progress. There is nothing new about appraisal and coaching. What is often disturbing is the emphasis placed on appraisal forms. Forms exist merely to ensure that the system is working, and working efficiently; they are the least important part of the process. Only the results, and the ability to communicate those results to supervisors, are of importance—and nothing else.

The Informal Appraisal

As manager you are constantly appraising each of your sales reps. You must decide whether to discharge the marginal sales rep and how much time you can properly spend with a new salesperson as against an older one. Your company is anxious to have your appraisal of how adequately the territory is being covered, how effectively the accounts are being served, and to what extent its objectives are being achieved. At the other end of the scale, the sales reps wonder what you, the boss, think of their performance. In making your appraisals, you continually use sales figures and other statistical data. They are specific and hit the bull's-eye so far as they go. You must, however, have other criteria which, though intangible, are equally important.

Let's list some of these other measures for appraisal.

1. *Sales reps must be willing to learn.* They must be anxious to improve themselves and receptive to instruction. When they lack this quality, you are wasting your time because such sales reps are incapable of growth and development.

2. *Sales reps should be happy in their job.* They should be enthusiastic, excited, and interested in each day's operations, well motivated, and able to keep their long-range objectives clearly in view.

3. *Sales reps should possess and use the ability to plan.* They should employ their time effectively; schedule the work for each day, week, and month; plan each interview carefully. They should think in terms of "next steps" in connection with each account.

4. *Sales reps should be able to conduct an effective sales interview.* They should know how to carry through effectively any part of a sales interview, including the interview with a receptionist. They should also be familiar with the use of the telephone where necessary, the art of giving demonstrations, the methods of closing orders, and the servicing of accounts.

Among the more important matters to be appraised in determining whether a sales rep is really moving ahead are the following:

1. Presence of strong motivation and a sound attitude toward the job and the future
2. A record of steadily increasing sales volume and steadily increasing earnings

3. Definite improvement in those areas in which the manager has felt coaching was required
4. Definite progress in the development of an increasing number of accounts with good potential
5. The continual development of new accounts
6. Willingness to assume responsibility, to handle tough situations in the territory without supervision, and to try new methods and ideas suggested by the boss
7. Ability to manage his or her personal life successfully

Managers appraise and coach sales reps each time they are in the field with them. Only thirty minutes may be involved, but the meeting does bring the sales rep and the manager closer together. When skillfully conducted, it presents the manager to the sales rep as a helper. Statistical material is reviewed, and the intangible qualities that make for success are discussed. The manager and the sales rep reach mutual agreement as to what must be done to achieve maximum results. The conclusions reached in such a discussion are sometimes reduced to writing by the manager, and a copy is sent both to the sales rep and to the manager's supervisor.

For the accurate appraisal of a sales rep, there is no substitute for direct field observation. In fact, a manager who sees his people in the field only once or twice a year cannot in good conscience appraise their performance. Every field contact, every review with a salesperson should conclude with some specific agreed-upon action to be taken before the next field contact. The key word is *action.* It is this insistence upon action following a field contact or review or informal appraisal that gives continuity to the entire supervisory and development process going on between the field sales manager and the sales rep. It also provides the most reliable appraisal tool.

When the field sales manager looks over four or five action sheets similar to the one shown in Figure 4-1 there must be some evidence that agreed-upon action was actually taken, that the sales rep was really trying to improve his performance. If there is no evidence, then there is a real question as to whether that salesperson is capable of development.

The keeping of some kind of an action record is an indication that continuity is being provided from one field contact to the next. This is important because without continuity the entire management function is fragmentized and loses its developmental aspect.

Figure 4-1. Example of an action sheet kept by a field sales manager.

Name of salesperson _____

Date _____

What has occurred with respect to the action to be taken following the last field contact? _____

_____

_____

_____

_____

What was accomplished on this field contact? _____

_____

_____

_____

_____

What specific action was agreed to be taken between this date and the next field contact? _____

_____

_____

_____

_____

What date was agreed upon for the next field contact? _____

_____

_____

_____

_____

Other comments: _____

_____

_____

_____

The Formal Appraisal

In contrast to informal appraisal, the formal appraisal covers a longer period—six months to a year—and requires the use of specially prepared forms. The latter can be quite formidable—to the point where they often confuse the field sales manager, who is more accustomed to selling and field work than to the intricacies of complex paperwork. Unfortunately, headquarters sometimes becomes so intent upon forms and their use that the real purpose of the appraisal is all but forgotten. The field sales manager must realize that the only value of a form lies in the information entered on it. If that information is put down carelessly or inaccurately, then the entire appraisal is worthless; and all the time spent in preparing, discussing, and analyzing it is not only wasted but may result in injury to the company and the sales rep. The manager should not be afraid of forms but should learn how best to work with them because of the part they play in the necessary periodic appraisal of each salesperson.

Because there are many different kinds of appraisals, I will attempt to deal only with the fundamental principles that the field sales manager must understand in order to be effective as an appraiser. It is not usually the manager's function to determine the form of appraisal. The printed forms and procedures are usually developed at headquarters, and the field sales manager is responsible only for carrying them out. Figure 4-2 represents a sales call appraisal form used by the 3M Corporation. Each company normally has confidence in the particular method of appraisal it employs. In some companies the sales reps perform self-appraisals, and their manager then prepares an independent appraisal. In others, the field sales manager appraises his salespeople and then discusses the appraisal with each sales rep. In still others, one or more persons confer with the field sales manager in preparing the appraisal. Regardless of the method employed, the field sales manager is the key person in the appraisal process; hence it is most important for the manager to be properly prepared for it.

Preparation for the formal appraisal is a continuing task. I suggest that you have a folder for each sales rep and that throughout the year you file in it all specific evidence that will substantiate your appraisal of a sales rep's performance. Such evidence is accumulated from correspondence, from telephone conversations, and from observations and experiences in the field with each sales rep. Without such tangible evidence the appraisal may possibly do more harm than good because, in the absence of proof, your sales reps may not accept what appears to them to be unjust criticism of some phase of their performance. Some companies require that a field sales manager back up every statement made with at least one specific example taken from actual experience with the sales rep. For example, the manager might say:

> Joe, you remember that when we called at Smith Brothers in Topeka, they were displeased with your handling of their complaint. We found the same problem when we called on Jones Manufacturing Company and the Adams Company of Wichita.

Preparation also involves recognition of the fact that you cannot and must not appraise a salesperson you do not know reasonably well. People who are new in the organization or whom you have rarely seen cannot be accurately appraised. As sales manager you should therefore plan and carry through enough field contacts with your sales reps that you will know them well enough to appraise them accurately.

Preparation for appraisal, finally, involves a true conception of the purpose of the appraisal. There are two major elements subject to appraisal—performance and personal qualifications. Performance should be appraised first. The sales rep's personal qualifications should be appraised only when they affect performance.

Among the questions frequently asked in the appraisal of sales performance are the following:

- Does the salesperson's performance result in a steadily upward trend in sales made and in their profitability?
- Does the rep's performance reflect steady improvement and strengthening of customer relations?
- Does the sales rep show a willingness and ability to handle problems?
- Has the rep been successful in developing new accounts?
- Does the rep's performance establish an ability to apply instructions and training? Has he or she made progress in achieving the objectives set earlier in the year?
- To what extent does the rep's performance manifest a basic integrity?
- How is the sales rep's performance affected by drive, moti-

Figure 4-2. Sales call appraisal form used by the 3M Corporation.

[front and back]

Ideas

Sales Call Appraisal

This is designed to help you to constantly improve yourself. By its quick use after each sales call you will be able to manage yourself to greater success & accomplishment

Job Responsibilities

Sales Volume

    Existing Accounts
    New Accounts
    Distribution

Account Penetration

New Account Development

Development of Distributor Reps

Sales Expense

Introduction of New Products & Programs

Communication & Administration

Self-Development

As Manager of a Market Area, a Sales Representative Should...

1. Analyze markets and customers.
2. Select target or key accounts.
3. Establish sales objectives.
4. Develop a plan.
5. Implement plan.
6. Control performance.

Form 19825 - C

3M Human Resources Development
Building 225-1N-10, 3M Center
St. Paul, MN 55144-1000

(continues on next page)

vation, and the pace of operations. (Does he or she lead or follow the manager?)

- Does the rep's performance benefit from an orderliness in handling office work and in maintaining personal possessions like home and car?
- How efficiently does the rep use time as indicated by the way in which he or she covers the territory and handles special problems that could be disruptive of routine?
- How is the rep's performance affected by such personal characteristics as appearance, speech, and intelligence?
- Does the rep obtain better results because of a familiarity with the job—that is, because of having superior knowledge

Figure 4–2. (cont.)

[inside]

How am I doing?
1. I need skill/knowledge for further development
2. I'm an average performer
3. I'm an above average performer
4. I excell & am innovative

Pre-Approach	1	2	3	4
Appearance				
Pre-call planning sheet				
Phone appointments				
Objective on every call				
Key buying influences identified				
Proper samples–tools				
Account card information				
Total potential analyzed				
Needs–wants–problems pre-determined				
Buyer styles determined				
Proposals used				
Successful outcome visualized				

Attention	1	2	3	4
Pre-planned				
Unique–creative				
Positive attitude				
Smile				

Involvement	1	2	3	4
Benefit claim used				
Third party evidence				
Open ended questions				
Needs–wants–problems uncovered–identified				
Good listening				
Notes taken				
Qualifying statement used to summarize				

Understanding & Agreement	1	2	3	4
Matching 3M products–systems & services to Customer needs–wants–problems				
Features tied to solutions				
Advantages tied to problems				
Benefits to satisfy wants–needs				
Demonstrations				
Third party				
Exhibits				
Checking questions				

Resistance	1	2	3	4
Stalls–real objections				
Anticipated resistance before raised				
Right answers				
Acknowledge the objection				
Answer with evidence				
Initial price vs. total cost explained				
Pencil sell				

Action	1	2	3	4
Buying signals–verbal–non-verbal recognized				
Checking questions used				
Variety of closes used				
Builds the order				
Sells the total system				
Sets the prospect–customer up for the next call				

Post-Call Analysis	1	2	3	4
Does a post call analysis after each call				
Uses this information for next sales call				
Notes–information entered on account records				
Innovate ideas for next call				

Follow-Up	1	2	3	4
Promises kept				
Training in use of products–systems				
Leads for other divisions–cooperating for growth				
Third party evidence documented				
Date of next call entered on calendar				
Orders per day				
Dollars per call				

demand the best from yourself

Reprinted with permission from the 3M Corporation, St. Paul, Minnesota.

of products, promotional or advertising programs, pricing, and policies?

When an appraisal program fails to achieve its objective, it is usually because the manager:

1. Appraises people he hardly knows.
2. Is in such a hurry that carelessness results.
3. Unconsciously exhibits bias in favor of or against a sales rep.
4. Employs incorrect standards of evaluation.
5. Gives undue weight to recent events.

6. Wants all his people to "look good' when the boss reviews the appraisals.
7. Uses flattering appraisals to win the favor of his reps.
8. Is afraid to give an adverse appraisal because he would have to discuss it with the salesperson in question.
9. Uses the appraisal to justify some other action he wishes to take, such as giving or refusing a raise in salary.

Here are a few suggestions as to how you can do a better job as field sales manager in helping your sales reps through sound appraisals. When appraisal time rolls around, you should devote your full time to the subject and not allow yourself to be rushed or distracted from the task. After becoming familiar with the forms and the instructions for their use, you should review the sales rep's job description with particular attention to specific standards of performance—for example, dollar or unit volume of sales, number of new accounts, sales by product line, number of calls, and so on. You should also study the objectives that were mutually agreed upon during the planning session, as well as any material you plan to use as documentation in the appraisal. Such review is important to ensure that the sales rep's performance is judged against the goals that were established for him or her. This job must be done thoroughly and thoughtfully not only because of the effect the appraisal will have on the sales rep's future but also because its accuracy or inaccuracy will be a reflection of your judgment as sales manager. The sales rep's performance in the period immediately preceding the appraisal is what counts; past judgments should not enter into the current appraisal. Finally, you should keep in mind that this is an evaluation of performance, not of personality—except to the extent that it affects performance—and that *the main purpose of the appraisal is to help the sales rep improve on performance.*

The Coaching Session

After you have made the appraisal, you then review it with the sales rep in a coaching session. You sit down and help the rep answer three very important questions: How am I doing? What do I do next? How can I do it better?

Let's take a look at coaching in its broadest sense. Essentially, it is a discussion of job performance between a sales manager and a sales rep that is a direct outgrowth of the preceding appraisal. It may involve commendation for a job well done or constructive criticism to correct a weakness that you have uncovered in your appraisal. Its purpose is to acquaint the sales rep with his or her strengths and weaknesses.

Coaching can occur in a variety of settings. For example, it may be a curbstone conference following a call on which you have accompanied the sales rep. Here you usually begin with a compliment. Although at times there is little to be complimentary about, you realize that the salesperson is under tension while working with you. Aware of being under observation and knowing that a comment on the performance is coming, the rep anticipates some criticism even before the interview begins. A bit of encouragement is in order, therefore, if the coaching is to be effective.

Some questioning about the interview just concluded will get the session moving. You may ask:

> What did you accomplish in the interview? What weaknesses do you think it showed? Given a second chance, what would you do to improve the interview? Did you notice this point I observed? Did you detect that reaction? What do you think of this idea for overcoming the objection that was raised?

Thus the sales rep is drawn into a discussion. You do not appear to be looking for faults; you are helping the sales rep to think through the problems. The results of this curbstone coaching session, including the agreement reached as to the next steps to be taken for the improvement of the sales rep's performance, will be noted later as part of your summary of the day's work.

Coaching may be initiated by the sales rep, triggered perhaps by some dissatisfaction or personal problem that is affecting his performance. This usually takes place in the field. Where possible, you should try to develop such a relationship with your people that they will advise you in advance of their desire for a session and of the subject to be discussed so that you can be prepared. Coaching may also be initiated by the manager. You may ask the sales rep to come to your office or to meet you in your hotel room or the hotel coffee shop. The purpose may be to advise on a special assignment or to correct some particular error of the sales rep.

Whenever the manager conducts an informal appraisal with a sales rep in the field, he follows it with a coaching session. This ties together the various points of the appraisal and gives direction to the entire effort. It brings the manager and the sales rep closer together and gives the salesperson a better understanding of what the manager is trying to do for him. In the case of the formal appraisal, it is imperative that it be followed by a coaching session. Any manager who has the responsibility for appraising a subordinate has a corollary responsibility to discuss that person's performance with him.

Among the definite benefits to be derived from a coaching session are the following:

- The sales rep learns exactly how she is doing; her strengths and weaknesses are emphasized.
- Plans for improvement of the sales rep's performance are produced.
- A strong personal relationship develops between the manager and the sales rep; consequently, the rep is willing to talk about his job performance and how it can be improved.
- The tensions and anxieties that exist when a sales rep does not know what his boss thinks of his performance, and hence in unable to plan with him for his growth and development, are reduced or eliminated.

Despite these advantages, the manager is often reluctant to have a coaching session with a sales rep. He finds it difficult to discuss performance with a salesperson face to face. Such a manager fails to understand the absolute necessity for coaching. The appraisal process has been compared to the diagnosis made by a doctor. It neither cures nor harms the patient; it merely tells the sick person what is wrong. This is always followed by a discussion with the patient and agreement upon a course of treatment. Similarly the manager, after telling the sales rep what he finds wrong with his or her performance, prescribes a remedy with the sales rep's approval.

Listed below are twelve suggestions for improving the coaching interview:

1. Agree on a time when both parties will be free from pressure. As manager you should allot a full day to the interview so that you are not watching the clock with an eye to some other appointment.

2. Select a place where there will be no interruptions—no telephone calls, mail deliveries, urgent messages, requests for "just a minute of your time." A hotel room may be best.

3. Give the salespeople you are planning to see advance knowledge of the purpose of the interview. They should know who made the appraisal and how the results were arrived at. They should be given an opportunity to outline what they hope to learn from the appraisal and coaching.

4. Because the purpose of the interview is to review and discuss the sales rep's performance and to help improve it, discuss performance first, mentioning personal qualities only when they affect that performance. *Concentrate your efforts on discovering opportunities for improvement rather than on baring weaknesses.* The best way to begin is by discussing the sales rep's results during the period covered by the appraisal and the methods used to produce those results. Then praise the rep's strengths, point out weaknesses, and jointly resolve, before the day is over, to outline a program aimed at the rep's growth and development.

At the beginning it is wise to stay with figures, statistical data about which there can be little disagreement. Otherwise questions may be raised to which there is no immediate answer. For instance, you might say:

> John, I note that your sales of product line B amount to only 2 percent of your total sales, whereas for the organization as a whole the figure is 10 percent. Do you know of any good reason for this? Perhaps there is no potential for that product in your territory, or you may have some questions about the quality of that product line.

Remember, you are a manager, not a psychologist or a psychoanalyst and that you tread on very dangerous ground when you try to probe someone's personality. This is one of the most serious mistakes made in coaching. Most of us do not possess the requisite professional skills, and we must never forget it. Job performance is the manager's province, and this is where you should concentrate your efforts.

5. Be positive in your approach to the coaching interview. Emphasize the strong points of the sales rep and support these by figures and examples. Make the sales rep feel that he is moving in the right direction, that he has been doing pretty well but is capable of doing even better.

6. As each subject is discussed, try hard to reach agreement with the rep on a course of action to improve the situation. It is not

enough for you merely to inform a rep that certain phases of his work need improvement. In this connection you must strive to avoid any argument or dispute with the sales rep that might result in hostility or resentment. The counseling interview should isolate the areas of agreement and include agreement on appropriate recommendations. Concerning points of disagreement, it is better to take no corrective action unless the matter is extremely vital—that is, unless it affects the salesperson's tenure or ultimate success with the company. Normally, there will be enough areas of agreement to provide the basis for a sound program for the development of the sales rep in the period ahead.

7. Wherever possible, be prepared to cite specific examples to substantiate your conclusions. Try collecting such evidence throughout the year, so that you are well supplied with sound proof by the time of the coaching interview.

8. If the sales rep convinces you that changes in the appraisal are in order, make them without delay. *A manager must be willing to listen to his salespeople and consider their point of view.* The sales rep must be made to feel that you are entirely fair and objective in your judgments as manager. However, the sales rep must be able to prove his case conclusively.

9. By means of the coaching interview, encourage your sales reps to think for themselves, to analyze their problems, and to develop sound solutions. This strengthens them, builds their self-confidence, and helps them to assume the necessary responsibility for the management of their territory. Managers are too often guilty of excessive paternalism; they give too much advice and do the salespeople's thinking for them.

10. *Make sure that the counseling interview always leads to a "next step" to be taken.* To achieve this end, it is important for both you and the sales rep to write down the principal areas in which the sales rep is going to try to improve and develop. There should be agreement also on the specific steps that are to be taken to achieve the objective in each area—for example, how the rep is going to improve sales of product line B.

11. Summarize the results of the coaching interview at its conclusion. The sales rep should leave the interview encouraged and optimistic. Avoid making either promises or threats, but show your moral support of the rep's determination to take responsibility and to depend on himself for success. Convince the sales rep that it is

your desire to help him in every possible way to achieve his objectives.

12. Make the agreed-upon objectives for the sales rep's development your objectives as well. Incorporate them into your program for action with that salesperson. Each field contact must be planned around these areas of the sales rep's development, and the success of each field contact can be measured in terms of the degree to which it moves the sales rep closer to these objectives.

The Sales Rep's Personal Life

To what extent should the field sales manager become involved in the personal life of the sales rep? Ordinarily, as I have pointed out, it should not concern you unless it affects the sales rep's performance or reflects unfavorably on the image of the company. In such a case a personal matter becomes a company matter as well, and you must deal with it promptly. Some excellent salespeople are careless about their appearance, but if this does not affect their performance, it need not concern you. In fact, you can nullify your efforts and lose rapport with your salespeople by trying to correct personal weaknesses when you should be concentrating upon the important, agreed-upon objectives for their development.

In general, management encourages field sales managers to involve the salesperson's spouse in the development program. For maximum achievement the sales rep must come home to a place where there is affection, encouragement, comfort, and relaxation. Sales reps do better when their families believe in them and are sold on the company and its policies. As manager you should know how the sales rep's spouse and family feel. One way to find this out is by inviting the sales rep and his or her spouse to dinner or, better yet, by getting yourself invited to their home for dinner. In an easy, informal setting you can direct the conversation to the spouse's goals and objectives and begin to understand how this person feels about being married to a sales rep. You can ask such questions as these:

> When you and your husband decided to accept this job as against other openings, you had certain reasons for making that decision. Now that you have been with the company awhile, do you feel that actual experience has borne out your original expectations?

You should discuss the couple's interests and their problems with them, yet avoid getting into the realm of personal problems unless one or the other of the two brings them up. You should listen carefully to what is said and reply pleasantly but honestly to any questions that indicate misgivings about the job and the sales rep's future. Of course, you should never discuss the company or its management personnel disparagingly, nor should you talk about other sales reps and their records.

The skillful manager will develop this close relationship with the sales rep and his or her spouse without ever permitting it to cloud recognition of the fact that he is the manager. The ideal relationship is one that is friendly but not intimate.

When a personal problem does affect the sales rep's performance or the company's image, then as manager you must act swiftly and effectively to deal with it and correct it. This calls for a prompt confrontation between you and the sales rep. The salesperson must be made to understand that no company can retain even a top-notch sales rep whose personal conduct is injurious to its business or reputation.

Coaching by Telephone or by Mail

Effective coaching can be done by telephone and even by mail. It is important, however, to determine the circumstances best suited to each medium.

Certainly a telephone call is ordinarily more effective than a letter, just as a personal interview is preferable to a telephone interview. There are certain matters than a good manager would discuss with a sales rep only in person and others that he might discuss in person or on the telephone, but never by letter. In each instance the manager must make the decision, and it can be important, particularly when it concerns the sales rep's willingness to follow the supervisor's suggestions.

Here's an example. You receive a memo from headquarters saying that sales rep Simpson uses the long-distance telephone excessively in calling the factory and that as manager you should correct this situation. Salesman Simpson lives some 200 miles from your office. Should you write Simpson, phone him, or talk to him personally when you next see him? The answer is a test of your empathy with and understanding of the sales rep. First of all, is improvement in use of the long-distance telephone one of the major, agreed-upon objectives that you and salesman Simpson are working together to achieve? If not, then this matter should not be treated as a major objective; it should not receive the same priority. Excessive telephoning is not a matter for which Simpson is likely to be discharged—he's too good a producer. What, then, is the best way to handle this matter?

Consider this possibility before sending him a letter or a memo. On the day the letter arrives, Simpson left home very early in the morning to resolve a sticky problem at an account some miles away. He then proceeded with other calls that unfortunately did not produce the results he had anticipated. He finally arrives home for dinner, hot, sweaty, dirty, worn out after a hard day, a little down in the mouth because of disappointments. At this moment there is nothing Simpson needs more than an arm on his shoulder and a pat on the back. Instead, he gets a letter telling him to cut down on long-distance telephone calls. Does this make him feel that you are really his helper, that you are trying to build him up and develop him? Or does he regard you as just another boss who doesn't see the good things a guy does but harps on every little thing that goes wrong?

It is doubtful whether a letter is the best way to coach a sales rep on relatively less important matters. The telephone is somewhat better in that the inflections of the human voice reveal more of the manager's feeling than does a sheet of paper with words on it. Yet even the phone may not fully convey your feeling that the subject is not terribly important. It probably will be best if you simply put a memo in his folder as a reminder to mention the matter to Simpson some afternoon during the next field contact when you are having a beer or a drink before dinner. Simpson can look you in the eye, listen to your voice, and get a sense of how you feel about long-distance calls—that is, although they are not of tremendous importance, it is desirable to control them.

The telephone may be used effectively in coaching a new sales rep by having her phone the manager daily during her first couple of weeks on the job to review what she has done, what problems she has run into, and what successes she has achieved. Of course, the manager will laud her for her successes, however small they may be. The telephone is also of value in following through with a senior salesperson with respect to some major objective. Let's assume the objective is to increase the sales of product line B and that this is also a broad company objective. The manager may phone the sales rep and ask her about her progress with this product line, what accounts have been interested in it, what obstacles are being encountered, and which new sales techniques are proving effective. In short, the manager asks a wide variety of questions to determine whether the sales rep is really making a proper effort to sell product line B and to show the sales rep that the boss considers this product line to be extremely important.

In summary, in situations where the telephone or a letter could be used for coaching, managers should consider very carefully whether to use either as well as *how* to use the medium selected for maximum effectiveness in developing their salespeople.

The Field Sales Manager's Supervisor

What is the field sales manager's role in the appraisal of sales reps for his boss? There are many ways in which appraisals are conducted, and I shall not attempt to describe each or decide which is best.

It is generally accepted that there is an advantage to involving at least one other person besides the manager in the appraisal before the coaching interview takes place. In many companies the field sales manager makes his appraisal of the sales rep and then discusses it with his boss. The advantage of this system is that the manager is required to thoroughly consider his appraisal of the sales rep's job performance and his opinion of the rep as a person. His boss will question him deeply on each item and probably raise some questions as to his judgment. Certainly he will receive guidance and help. In addition, this conference should result in agreement between the manager and his boss on the appraisal as it will be discussed with the sales rep. The sales rep, knowing of the joint work that went into the appraisal, is more likely to accept it. Since the manager's boss was involved in making the appraisal, he or she should be advised of the outcome of the coaching interview and should receive a copy of the agreed-upon objectives that will form the basis for the work the manager will do with the sales rep during the period ahead.

Motivation Techniques

Motivating your salespeople is one of your most important responsibilities as field sales manager. To be sure, the word *motivation* can be frightening, particularly to a newly appointed field sales manager. It simply means that *you must inspire your people to want to do better*—to want to grow and develop. Sales reps must realize that the manager and the company want them to grow and develop and will do everything possible to help. This is a pretty big order, especially when you consider how widely individuals differ in personality.

Sales reps use great skill in dealing with the various purchasing people they call on, and their success depends upon their ability to understand them, their needs, and their problems. But this responsibility of the sales rep is not nearly as exacting as your obligation to understand your salespeople, their problems, and their needs. I have already pointed out that the success of the manager and the sales rep depends upon their ability to work together as a team. But how can the sales rep cooperate in this effort if he or she is unhappy with the job, dislikes the manager, or feels that the company is being exploitive? The responsibility for motivating the sales rep rests squarely on the shoulders of the manager. The success of the manager, the sales rep, and the company will depend on how well this responsibility is met.

The new district or field sales manager can perform no task of greater value than to go into the field at once and get acquainted with every one of his salespeople and perhaps with their spouses too. Most people in top management agree that the first job of the newly appointed field sales manager is to make sure that each of his sales reps feels that the company's interests, the manager's interests, and the sales rep's interests are the same. Sales reps must be made to understand that their achievements are necessary to the manager's success, and that it is in the manager's personal interest to help the salespeople in every way possible.

Where motivation is concerned, you must concentrate on the individual and for the moment forget about sales, quotas, policies, and performance. For instance, should you learn that a sales rep feels the need for recognition within her community, you may be able to motivate her by having an article about some accomplishment of hers published in a local paper. Or you may motivate a rep by showing him how to plan his work better so that he is relieved of the tension and pressure that have been making him irritable at home and inefficient in the field. You may be able to help a sales rep improve his chances of promotion. You may, by some special recognition at a sales meeting, help build his morale. In short, by talking informally with your salespeople and their families, it is possible for you to learn how to help your sales reps find real satisfaction, happiness, and a sense of achievement in the job as well as merely a way of earning money. While earnings must, of course, be adequate, they are rarely the primary motivational factor in a sales rep's success.

I must emphasize that the job of motivating sales reps is best done in the field and not from an office. It is a personal operation and cannot be handled by forms, contests, letters, or phone calls. As field sales manager you must realize that each of your sales reps watches you carefully and observes everything about you—your manners, habits, language, dress, attitudes, and so on. To exert any influence over your salespeople, you must have their respect. To earn this, you must:

- Have character. It's important that your sales reps and their spouses admire your character and the standards by which you live.
- Be capable of doing hard physical and mental work without complaint.
- Be completely frank and open under all circumstances.
- Be the champion of your company when you are with your people. At the same time, be *their* champion. Remember, always deal promptly with their complaints when you are at headquarters.
- Be willing to take the risks involved in letting the sales rep control the interview when the two of you call on a customer together.
- Build up your sales reps before customers at every opportunity.
- Help your sales reps overcome obstacles.
- Be calm, confident, smiling, and composed when in the presence of a sales rep.
- Set the pace when with a sales rep.
- Be fair, yet firm, in your dealings with your sales force.

How do you know whether you are motivating your salespeople? Count yourself successful when:

- The sales rep says *we,* not *you, I,* or *they* (the company) when discussing a business matter.
- The sales rep has reached a genuine agreement with you on common goals or objectives and works with you toward their achievement.

- The sales rep brings his problems to you for help without fear of criticism.
- The sales rep knows that you will listen patiently to what she has to say.
- The sales rep feels free to communicate with you in person, by phone, or by mail.
- The sales rep feels completely at ease when making a call in your presence.

To elaborate a bit on this important subject, it may be said that motivation is achieved when, first, you manifest to the sales rep your complete confidence in him. You do not check closely on all his activities. You are not a policeman or a social worker but a sales manager, and it is not your function to police your sales rep to make sure that he is working or that he is not drinking too much or beating his wife. If the rep needs a policeman or a social worker, then perhaps the company needs another salesperson. *Your job as manager is to work with sales reps who want to do well,* accelerate their progress, and guide them toward success.

Second, motivation is achieved when you give the sales rep real responsibility. It is risky to delegate an important responsibility to a salesperson. If a sales rep is given the responsibility of holding a dissatisfied account or closing a big order and fails, then you as manager will have to take the blame. Yet it is a risk that must be taken if you hope to develop that rep.

Third, the sales rep is motivated when he achieves success in some area and receives your congratulations. Having overcome his fear of failure and having enjoyed the sweet taste of success, he is interested in going after more of it.

Fourth, the sales rep is motivated when he receives recognition in his job and in his private life; when he is given an important assignment at a sales meeting and gains the recognition of his peers; when some fine order he has obtained is published in the company house organ; when he knows that he is regarded by his family, his friends, and his customers as a top sales rep.

Fifth, motivation exists when the sales rep feels that he is on the team. Frequently ask his opinion and value his views on various business problems. Finally, full motivation is achieved when you and the sales rep have agreed-upon objectives. The sales rep knows what you are trying to do to help him and also knows exactly what is expected of him.

What I have been saying is that the motivation of a sales rep rests largely on the skill and ability of the field sales manager. Did you ever notice that the people most eager to play bridge are the better players, that those most highly motivated to play golf are the fine golfers? Similarly, the salespeople who are most highly motivated to sell are those who, with the manager's help, have become the very best sales reps.

But what about the sales rep who does not respond to your managerial efforts? Before passing judgment, you should critically examine your relationship with the individual to make certain that the fault is not your own. If you conclude that you are not responsible for the sales rep's failure to respond, it must follow that the sales rep is not capable of development. It is useless to butt your head against a stone wall trying to develop people who either are incapable of development or just don't want to make the necessary effort. Sales reps can be divided into two classes: those capable and those incapable of development. As field sales manager, you should spend most of your time with those who do show possibilities. You will have scant time for the others.

As manager you may call someone who shows little promise of development into your office occasionally for a short conference so that that rep will feel some identification with the company. Or you may see the rep occasionally for the primary purpose of contacting important accounts in the territory rather than for personal development work. If the rep in question is doing a pretty good sales job without help, you may reach an agreement with him to the effect that, since he doesn't want to be on the team, he can go his own way so long as he achieves his specific objectives with respect to accounts sold, products sold, sales volume, and profitability. Any failure to meet these objectives will necessitate his replacement. In any event, all reps in this category should be slated for replacement sooner or later. There may be good reasons for not discharging them immediately, but there is no justification for wasting your valuable time and money in trying to perform the impossible with them. Since it is your primary function as manager to develop sales reps, you must spend your time with those who, however imperfect, *want* to develop and improve.

To ensure the sound growth of the company, to move people up through the organization (assuring high morale), an important objective of every field sales manager should be to produce at least one promotable person per year. There may not be a place for that person immediately, but it does mean that if and when there is an opening, there will be a competent person available to fill it.

Motivation Through Contests

Many companies have found that contests are a strong motivating force within their sales organizations. Where a contest is ordered by headquarters, field sales managers merely carry out the instructions given them and supervise its conduct within the assigned area. If as field sales manager you yourself initiate the contest, you must consider a number of factors.

First, a contest is no substitute for a good sales management effort. Second, a contest has drawbacks as well as benefits. It may interfere with good planning and proper territorial coverage by encouraging sales reps to chase around their territories trying to sell a particular product or a certain class of trade for which the contest offers a special reward. This will result in a serious falling off of business after the contest is concluded, and it will require special efforts to get sales reps "back on the beam" in terms of sound planning and territorial management. Further, it may cause reps to overlook important opportunities for business while pursuing the objectives of the contest. The value of the contest may ultimately prove insignificant in comparison with the losses due to disruptions in normal planning and coverage.

Third, the rewards offered in a contest must be substantial and significant. A sales organization with high earnings levels normally will not respond to a contest in which the rewards are small relative to earnings. Very few field managers can offer prizes and bonuses sufficient to interest people who are earning over $50,000 annually. Fourth, contests should not be overly long. They should not disrupt good working habits and methods. They should tie in with the major objectives of the sales reps and the district or region. They must be carefully and thoroughly planned and executed, preferably by someone with considerable experience.

Discharging Salespeople

One of the field sales manager's most difficult and distasteful jobs is that of firing sales reps who are not pulling their weight. In some cases the manager has a relationship with the salespeople which makes it extremely difficult to tell them that they are "through." Then again, the manager may feel that the salesperson's failure will be interpreted by headquarters as a managerial failure. Or it may be a case of borderline performance; the manager is reluctant to give up on the individual. Huge sums are lost every year in most sales organizations because some reps are kept on their jobs much longer than they should be.

As manager you must recognize that you are often in the position of a gambler sitting at a poker table. Your ante (recruitment and employment costs) is in the pot before you see any cards. With each card dealt you bet more money and gradually see what kind of a hand you are getting (what kind of a person you have employed). There comes a time when you must decide whether the hand is worth holding or whether you had better turn the hand down and take your loss before it becomes greater.

All too often you may be tempted to justify the retention of a rep in terms of some isolated instance, such as one good order the sales rep secured, even though all the factors relating to the rep's general performance are unfavorable. This kind of sales rep is very much like the "dub" golfer who is about ready to throw his clubs away when he gets a beautiful drive right down the center of the fairway. He really is no better a golfer than he was before—it was just a lucky shot. The same thing is true of the "dub" sales rep who also can get a lucky break. As manager you must have sound criteria for determining when a sales rep is no longer a good investment in time and money. One excellent yardstick is the degree of effort put in by the rep and his or her actual success in attaining objectives. This sound measurement takes much of the guesswork out of the question of when to retain sales personnel and when to let them go. There must be some evidence of progress, however small. When there is no apparent effort or progress, you know that the rep is no longer a good investment.

This measurement is best used during field contacts when you are observing the sales rep in action. For instance, assume that one agreed-upon objective is that the rep increase sales of product line B, the company's most profitable line. The company obtains 25 percent of its volume from this line, but the rep has been obtaining only 5 percent of her sales from it. You have taught her sales techniques and worked with her in the field, and she has promised to put these newly learned methods into practice. If, on subsequent contacts, you note that the rep has been trying and that product line B now constitutes 10 percent of her sales, there is reason to keep on working with her. On the other hand, if subsequent contacts show that she has done nothing to improve her sales of this important product line, it is likely that she is also disregarding the other development work that was done with her. If, in addition, her sales volume is unsatisfactory, it is probably wise to discharge her.

There is also a psychological angle to a sales rep's inadequate performance. The sales rep knows she is doing poorly and is probably very unhappy about it. This unhappiness manifests itself in her work as well as in her home life. This woman, who probably has talents that would be useful in another type of work, is employed at a job for which she is obviously unfitted and which is making her miserable. It is unfair as well as unwise to keep this individual at a job where she is a misfit. Rather, she should be encouraged to seek a type of employment at which she can hope to succeed. With this in mind, you can approach the sales rep and discuss her separation from the company in the knowledge that you are actually helping her.

In the case of a newly employed sales rep, you must observe his grasp of the job and his progress very closely. Many companies consider a newly employed salesperson on trial during his first two or even three years. As one executive put it: "The new salesman is like a runner in a hurdle race. He must successively jump one hurdle after another during his two-year probationary period [the first hurdle is the interview when he applied for the job]. If he kicks over a hurdle, he is out of the race."

Dealing With the Veteran Sales Rep

While not directly involved with the subject of separation, there should be some discussion of a problem faced by most field sales managers: what to do about older sales reps who are unable to carry their share of the load any longer. In some cases top management protects these senior reps, and the field sales manager has no authority to alter their status with the company. Yet the field sales manager is given a quota of business to secure, and must have the full sales potential of the older rep's territory in order to make good at his own job.

Occasionally, top sales management dictates the procedure to be followed, and nothing is left to the discretion of the field sales manager. But for those field managers who do have some say in such matters the problem is essentially one of fairness both to the veteran sales rep and to the company. On the one hand, the manager is morally obligated to protect the older sales rep in recognition of his contribution to the company over many years. On the other, the manager must consider the interests of the company and its stockholders and safeguard the business in the territory.

There are a number of possible solutions to this problem. Each situation must be judged on its own merits. In all cases, though, a personal interview with the sales rep in question should precede any action. Among the solutions that have worked out well in practice are the following:

1. The older sales rep is assigned to the office for staff work, and a younger person takes over his territory.

2. The older sales rep is allowed to keep as many of his key accounts as he can service properly, and the remainder of the territory is turned over to a junior sales rep who will inherit the entire territory when the older salesperson reaches retirement age.

3. The older sales rep accepts a junior salesperson to work under him and assist in the coverage of his territory, as he may direct. The cost of the junior sales rep during the first year is borne by the company, with an increasing percentage of the cost being charged to the veteran sales rep each year until his retirement.

4. The older sales rep is given special sales work at reduced but adequate compensation, and his place is taken by a younger sales rep.

5. The older salesperson is retired early, and this extra cost is absorbed by the company to maintain the sales volume and profit level in the territory affected.

5

The Control Function

As field sales manager you are in control of your job when:

1. As a result of sound appraisal (formal and informal) and progress toward agreed-upon objectives, you know how to improve performance.
2. You apply this knowledge to improved planning.

One of the more important duties of management is to be in control of the operation assigned to it. As a manager, you assign a part of your responsibility to other people; yet you are held accountable by your supervisors for the entire operation. You cannot excuse failure by blaming those under you. It is expected that you will be in control at all times and will see to it that the entire job gets done properly.

In the cycle of management, which is discussed in Chapter 1, control is an important part of steps three and four. Having set objectives and planned to do something, you, the manager, through your salespeople, proceed to carry out the plans in step two. You must then be vigilant to control the job by constantly asking yourself: "How is this operation going? What needs to be done now to keep it running smoothly and to strengthen any weak spots?" When you know the answers to these questions daily or at least weekly, and when you react to these answers with positive action, you are in control of your job.

Controls are effective only when they transmit important information quickly. A control must instantly shut off a machine or turn in an alarm in a time of danger. Controls fail when they are overly complex, voluminous, and detailed. They may be compared to traffic lights. It would be utterly ridiculous to place copies of a city's traffic code at each corner. A simple red, yellow, and green light system provides adequate and effective control. Many executives have actually adopted this idea and use the same colors to indicate situations under their jurisdiction. When a sales rep is performing well, the light is green. When the controls show a yellow light, the manager seeks more detailed statistical and other information to get to the bottom of the problem. And when a red light flashes, he knows a crisis exists. Traffic is stopped and immediate action is required. So here I am going to talk about simple controls that quickly flash to the manager a picture of progress, or the lack of it, in each area of his overall responsibilities.

What must the manager control? To some people the word *control* denotes control of others. I suggest here that you think of the term as a system that enables you to be in control of those tasks your superiors expect you to perform, and those tasks that you must perform for and with your salespeople so that both you and they can achieve your respective objectives. The following list informs you as to what you must control and what you must do to attain such control:

1. Your job description. You will want a control that tells you how you are doing with respect to each task listed.
2. The agreed-upon objectives you and your boss have drawn up, which are more specific than the job description. You will want to know how you are doing with respect to these goals, and the control system should tell you this.
3. The agreed-upon objectives that each of your sales reps has drawn up with you. Controls must tell you what you have to do to help each of your salespeople toward their objectives.
4. Statistical material from headquarters. These data enable you to be in control of your job by telling you whether any new problems have arisen that must be dealt with promptly.

As manager you are in control of your job when you are doing something effective about each responsibility assigned to you whether it is being performed by you personally or by some other person to whom you have delegated it. You are in control when you see and react to "red lights" promptly and effectively. One of the greatest benefits to be derived from the effective use of controls is that you have more time to devote to important things. Most of us feel inundated by the mass of work we have to do. What shall we do first? Some things are obviously more important than others. Controls can tell us, or at least help us to decide, which matters urgently require attention and which can wait. But a good control system can go beyond this and actually help in the allotment of time for every necessary task. A good system almost talks, saying: "You agreed to perform task *A,* and now you must find the time to get that job done." Then it helps in finding the appropriate time. In short, *a good control system won't let the manager forget anything.* Of course, for controls to be of any value, you *must* find the time to examine and study them. If you are a manager with ten reps under you, you must set aside at least an hour or two each week for this purpose if you are to be really in control of your management job.

The Field Sales Organization and Electronic Equipment

To help make your control system as modern and as efficient as possible, you will no doubt want to investigate whatever electronic equipment fills the bill. The use and extent of the use of electronic equipment varies greatly with different organizations. In some cases the entire program or system for using such equipment in sales and marketing originates at headquarters. Where there is no central program, the field sales manager may buy some equipment to help in doing the job better. In some cases it is the individual salesperson who may decide to purchase a portable computer or cellular phone, or the field sales manager may request and receive authority to purchase and pay for such equipment.

I am simply pointing out that the electronic age is upon us and there is increasing evidence that the use of such equipment by field sales managers and their salespersonnel is advantageous.

Well, then, let's see just when, where, and how the various kinds of electronic equipment may be used. Bear in mind that your main job as field sales manager is still in the field developing salespeople (getting them to be at least as good as you are and, hopefully, promotable). And the main job of the salespeople is still in the field developing accounts (getting accounts to *prefer* to do business with them and their company).

Yet there is growing pressure on the field sales manager to spend more time on desk work: correspondence, telephone calls, territory analysis, planning field trips, getting out reports, going over all kinds of figures, lots of paperwork—all necessary to perform the job. At the same time, salespeople, in addition to spending full time out in the field, are expected to fill out route sheets, daily reports, weekly reports, precall planning sheets, and postcall analysis sheets. Just when does the sales rep do this *formi*dable part of the job?

There is nothing new about all this. It has always taken a great deal of valuable time to produce necessary information and to put it into usable form. But to assist this effort electronic equipment is now available and the results have been tremendous. Figure 5-1 gives an idea of the many uses to which electronic equipment can be put.

As field sales manager, you can perform a valuable service by determining the optimum use of such equipment in your area of responsibility and by communicating this information to your supervisors.

In this chapter, I deal with the kind of information that has always been necessary if the field sales manager and the sales reps are to operate efficiently. But now, instead of having this information stored on cards, in files, or in loose-leaf notebooks, you can have access to it simply by "pressing a button." In short, use of the PC and the cellular phone together with the portable fax machine allow the field sales manager to spend more time on the main job, and the salespeople to spend more time on their priorities.

Organizing the Control Function

In order to achieve the benefits outlined and to enjoy the grand feeling that comes with being in control of the job, it is important that you set up certain signaling devices. These will vary with the special needs of each manager as well as with the nature of the business and the functions that the manager's people are expected to perform. A different kind of control is needed for the sales rep who details grocery stores than for the sales rep who sells machine tools. I am outlining here one of the many ways in which control may be achieved. Although it has worked well in practice, undoubtedly other methods would work as well or perhaps better. In any case, you should proceed as follows:

1. Make a list of every task for which you are responsible. Include all items in your job description plus any other specific responsibilities delegated to you by your supervisors.

2. Divide this list into those tasks you must perform personally (make a folder for each one), and those tasks to be delegated to sales reps or to people in your branch office (make a folder for each such person and file in it the specific tasks delegated to that person).

3. The original list should now contain only those tasks you must do yourself plus the names of persons accountable to you for delegated tasks.

4. Throughout the year periodically review the contents of each person's folder with him or her. With a sales rep, this will usually be during a field contact, or, in the case of a secretary, in your branch office.

5. Put into the personal folders such items as you will want to discuss with these people when you are with them. This will include matters having to do with their achievements or failures with respect to any delegated responsibilities. In many instances you will make quick notes on a scratch pad and drop these in the folder. Matters may occur in correspondence with headquarters, with customers and prospects, or even with one of your sales reps. Bear in mind that you are at your maximum effectiveness when you are with the salespeople in the field. Therefore, important matters usually will not be handled by mail or phone except in an extreme emergency.

6. Divide and group the remaining tasks, those you have decided to perform yourself, as follows:

   a. On one sheet list all tasks to be performed monthly or more frequently and place an X under the day (or days) of the month when that particular task is to be performed. At the same time enter the task under the same date in your diary (see Figure 5-2).

   b. On a second sheet list all tasks you are to perform less often than monthly (see Figure 5-3) and place an X under the month when each task is to be performed. This sheet need only be prepared once a year. Enter each of these tasks under the appropriate month in your diary.

(text continues on page 104)

Figure 5–1. Electronic sales tools and some of their uses.

Computers (now available in portable laptop models with capabilities similar to those of larger desktop models). They provide:

Fast access to customer lists, sorted by:

- Location (saves travel time between calls)
- Zip code
- Name (alphabetically)
- Products used
- Corporate size
- Volume of purchases possibly by product

Additional customer information:

- Next step to be taken and date of next call
- Date when next business will be placed
- Names and titles of all contacts and personal information on each
- Phone and FAX numbers
- Last quotations and discounts given

Fast access to data on salespersons:

- Agreed-upon objectives of each
- Areas for improvement for each
- Next steps to be taken for each
- Date of next field contact
- Date of next review

Fast access to field sales manager's direct responsibilities:

- Overall agreed-upon objectives
- Percent of each objective obtained (kept current)
- Next steps to be taken and when
- Operation of a branch office
- Accounts where field sales manager is directly involved

Figure 5–1. (cont.)

Word processors. They permit:

- The writing of quotations with standard paragraphs for terms and conditions, descriptions of products, and other standard information
- The maintenance of inventory lists with the capacity for quick daily updates
- The maintenance of detailed price sheets with quick update and retrieval capacity

Spread sheet programs for fast computations on complex computations.

FAX machines (portable FAX machines are available for use with car phones). They can:

- Send data and drawings between remote locations by phone.
- Send speed written communications between field sales manager and salespeople and between field sales manager and headquarters.
- Transmit purchase orders and extensive data lists with accuracy.
- Receive written confirmation.

Computers and FAX machines can both be used to transmit sales reports and/or receivables if a salesperson has responsibility for collections; also to transmit credit information.

Modems permit connections between computers and computer terminals for quick remote update of data. Information can be transferred on off-hours at lower phone rates and without disturbing the daily use of equipment.

Cellular telephones can keep salespeople in touch with their office and customers regardless of the salesperson's location. There are also "beepers" that can receive short messages almost anywhere within the continental United States.

Overhead projectors and/or video computers can be used both to prepare illustrative material and to revise it. Video is a help in showing how equipment works and its rates of production.

---

c. Once a month prepare a new sheet listing every task you will perform during the ensuing month, including field contacts with sales reps and contacts with others. Include a posting of all items from Figure 5-3 where there are X's under the current month. Thus you will have a complete list of tasks to be performed during the current month, and you will have assigned a time for performing each.

7. Each day review tasks scheduled for the following day so that folders will never be forgotten. Take out the folder covering each task to help you prepare for it.

8. Make sure your diary governs all use of your time for performing this control function so that you don't assign the same time to more than one task.

9. Arrange as much uninterrupted time for your office duties as possible. There should be a time for phone calls, a time for conferences, and a time to do this important control job without interruption.

10. Make certain that you are doing something about every task for which you have accepted personal responsibility and that you are reviewing your sales reps' performance of delegated tasks.

Controlling the Individual Sales Rep

Figures 5-4 and 5-5 suggest one simple method of controlling the progress of each sales rep. Of course, these forms will vary with the business or the particular sales functions. I include them as models to stimulate thinking with regard to the kind of controls best suited for each manager's purpose. Figure 5-4 tells the manager how many field contacts were planned with the salesperson and how many were actually made, the interval between these contacts, and whether another field contact is indicated at this time. It also lists the agreed-upon objectives for the development of that sales rep during the current year and shows how and when the manager has dealt with each such objective while on field contacts with the sales rep. It may contain refresher notes for the manager on the sales rep's progress, or lack of it, with respect to each objective. Figure 5-5 is a statistical record that will enable the manager to quickly appraise the sales rep's progress. These figures may be supplied by data processing

Figure 5–2. Sample monthly control sheet kept by a manager.

ACTIONS TO BE TAKEN THIS MONTH

MAY 199—

	1	2	3	S 4	5	6	7	8	9	10	S 11	12	13	14	15	16	17	S 18	19	20	21	22	23	24	S 25	26	27	28	29	30	31
Review controls	X								X							X							X							X	X
Review target accounts				X													X		X												
Review product line B sales												X														X					
Plan field contacts					X							X							X							X					
Recruitment and interviews			X							X							X							X							
Plan and issue bulletins					X							X							X							X					
Correspondence	X								X							X							X						X		
Plan calls on special accounts	X								X							X							X						X		
Set up control for next month																							X			X					
Work schedule for product manager	X															X										X					
Work schedule for sales training					X				X													X									
Review branch office operation												X							X							X					
Expense study															X																
Boss—conference and field work	X													X																	
Solar Mfg. Co.	X																				X							X			
General Mfg. Co.	X														X													X			
Acme Mfg. Co.															X						X							X			
Jim						X	X																								
Joe								X																							
Alice													X	X																	
Mike																				X	X										
Bill																										X	X				

Figure 5-3. Sample yearly control sheet for manager's use.

Tasks to be Performed Less Often Than Monthly
199—

	Jan.	Feb.	Mar.	Apr.	May	June	July	Aug.	Sept.	Oct.	Nov.	Dec.
Annual budget											X	
Appraisal of each sales rep					X							
Annual planning sessions											X	X
Quarterly progress review	X			X			X			X		
Management idea folder	X		X		X		X		X		X	
Sales meetings		X			X			X			X	
Staffing requirements						X						X
Sales forecast												X
Appraisal by boss								X				X
Product manager conference		X										
Marketing manager conference			X						X			
Training manager conference				X						X		

Figure 5-4. Sample field contact record.

Control						Date Accepted								

Objectives _____ by Sales Rep _____ Rep: _____

Year 199_

Date sales rep became a senior   Territory: _____

Date contact planned:													

Date contact made:													

Date of field contact on which rep was helped toward objective	List of objectives to be achieved during the current year to assure the fullest development of the representative. This list may have objectives added or removed during the year.
	1. $_____ of sales.
	2. Improve planning of interview and of territorial coverage.
	3. Solve problem of getting to higher echelons.
	4. Improve sales of product line B.
	5. Improve sales to trade class No. 6.

equipment at headquarters or in other ways devised for specific situations.

Thus the control system is simple, yet effective, and easily understood by the busy field sales manager who hasn't the time to pore over voluminous and complex figures. Two sheets of paper similar to Figures 5-4 and 5-5 can be placed in each sales rep's folder. If they are kept up-to-date by the manager or his secretary and studied prior to each field contact with the sales rep, the manager will always be in control of that salesperson's work. Controls of this kind are usually reviewed by field sales managers weekly to catch any "yellow light" that points up the need for more careful study of that sales rep's work. A well-devised control system should not require more than one to two hours attention a week. It must keep the manager well informed about every phase of the job without riveting him to his desk and curtailing his activity as a *field* sales manager.

The Field Sales Manager's Office

The physical facilities provided for the sales manager's office work—his control and communications center—vary widely. In some cases he may operate out of his home, where he has set aside space for a

Figure 5-5. Sample data sheet kept by a field sales manager on a rep.

Control 199—														

Name of Salesperson _____

Objective or quota _____

Objective or quota previous year _____

Best year $ _____   year _____

Training cost

199 ___ $ _____

199 ___ $ _____

Month	Prev. Year	Jan.	Feb.	Mar.	Apr.	May	June	July	Aug.	Sept.	Oct.	Nov.	Dec.
Sales vol. cumulative													
Sales vol. monthly													
Cum. ahead or below previous year													
Cumulative % of objective													
Cumulative % prev. year													
Earnings current cum.													
Cum. ahead or below previous year													
No. of orders													
No. of new accounts													
No. of interviews													
No. of days worked													
No. of days not worked													

Compensation current basis	Line	Number of orders obtained for important product lines											
	A												
Date — Amt./Month	B												
	C												
	D												
		Progress with important target accounts											
	Amco												
	Balco												
	Derix												
	Porto												
	Resco												
	Tinor												

desk and files, while in other instances he is provided with a district office. The district office may be very simple or the manager may be given a secretary or secretary-stenographer. In a more sophisticated arrangement, the manager may have a sales correspondent in addition to a secretary and even two or three assistants. In some branch offices the field sales manager has a staff for handling local warehousing of company products and for routine or special services to customers. Such an office may house technical specialists who work with the sales manager and his staff. Consequently, my comments are necessarily general and must be adapted to the individual manager's situation.

Because the average field sales manager has had little or no experience in running an office, he often finds this part of the job frustrating. His supervisors may have given him little or no instruction in office management, and he gets bogged down in a mass of office work, which impedes performance of his true function as a field sales manager. Let's begin by considering the real purpose of a field manager's office. Why is it at all necessary to have an office out in the field, considering the highly sophisticated machinery of the modern headquarters office? Certainly, the field office is not needed as a "parking place" for the field sales manager. We have already seen that the manager's job is performed mainly in the field with the sales force. In fact, when the office keeps him from performing this primary job, it loses its value as a working tool. Further, if the office keeps the manager nailed down to a desk much of the time, it would be more economical and efficient to keep field managers at headquarters rather than scatter them in small branch offices throughout the country. There is a valid objective in setting up a branch office out in the field and away from headquarters. An army officer on the battlefield with his men has only a walkie-talkie for his "office." He must be in constant communication both with his superiors and with his soldiers. This probably illustrates the primary function of the branch office; it is a communications center and a control center. It need be very little more. Unfortunately, this is sometimes forgotten by the field sales manager's supervisors who burden him with voluminous paperwork, which makes of him a field *office* manager rather than a field *sales* and *sales rep* manager.

Normally, however, the field sales manager's work can be so organized that most of his time is spent out in the field, using the office for support as a communications and control center. A portable dictating machine for use on field trips will help him tremendously. In fact, no investment made by top management will turn out more profitable. The material dictated by the manager can be transcribed at the branch office or sent to headquarters for transcription and distribution in accordance with instructions. Such equipment enables the manager to take immediate action with respect to matters discussed with a sales rep in the field or with a customer or prospect. Not only will the reporting be more accurate, having been done on the spot rather than from notes made on the backs of envelopes or on scraps of paper, but the manager need only consider the matter *once* and then dictate the findings. Otherwise, you must not only decide what action is to be taken while in the field, but you must also repeat the entire operation when you return to your office and base your dictation on memory and hurried notes.

Dictating equipment also saves much time in the office. As the manager goes through the mail or concludes a telephone conversation or conference, he can immediately dictate the essence of what was said or done. The job of "writing up" or "recalling" what occurred is not hanging over his head. He is free from this pressure because the record was made at the time of the action. Other pieces of equipment that enable the field sales manager to be more effective are the portable or laptop computer, the fax machine available in portable form, and the cellular phone. Such tools permit the job to be done out in the field while the manager is performing as a communicator and as a keeper of ongoing records needed for good management of the job.

It is not often that a field sales manager is assigned an administrative assistant or a full-time secretary. Nevertheless there is no question but that some help is necessary: help in providing accurate information when needed; in handling cassettes (discs, tapes) quickly and efficiently; in keeping control folders and files up-to-date and ready for immediate use when required; in taking phone calls when the field sales manager is in the field; in making some appointments; and in referring matters to the field sales manager in the field or following through with headquarters so that the office is truly a control and communications center. Such a person may have a number of other responsibilities and even perform similar duties for other executives in the same office.

If avoidable, the manager should *never handle a piece of paper twice.* When going through the mail, he should have his dictating machine at hand. With the first reading of each piece of mail, he should take whatever action is required and then file it.

In reviewing statistics, he should go over the figures carefully, then dictate memos, suggested action, directives, notes to himself, and the like so that, once having reviewed the figures, he need not go over them again. Letters requiring a reply should be answered at the time of reading, if at all possible. Often it is not necessary to write a complete reply to a letter; it will suffice simply to pencil on the bottom of the letter some brief remark such as, "O.K., Tom"; "Will handle when in Moline on May 10th"; or "Will do, Tom." The original letter can then be returned to the sender with the notation. This is especially valuable when no record of the correspondence is necessary, and it also avoids cluttering up the files. Dates can be entered in the manager's diary, and any action to be taken can be noted in the folder of the sales rep involved. When the manager reviews this folder in preparation for a field contact with the sales rep, the memo will appear as a reminder to him to take care of the matter.

Many field sales managers are dismayed on their return from

the field by the mountain of mail, reports, and statistics awaiting them. The suggestions made here are calculated to ease this situation by providing some guidance to the manager in establishing efficient office routines. When the manager is about to dictate, he should have his secretary bring him all the material he will need for his dictation. All too often the manager has to get up and look for more information or have his secretary dig it up. It is far more expeditious to get all the material together first so that the dictation can proceed without a hitch. The manager should regularly allot an uninterrupted period to communications. Similarly, he should set aside a definite period to exercise control. He may decide that every Friday morning will be devoted to the study of each sales rep's performance to determine whether any action should be taken. He should permit no interruptions during this period. Thus in a relaxed manner and with proper concentration, the manager can review both his own performance and that of his salespeople, determine the next course of action, and set it in motion.

A brief anecdote will illustrate why managers should understand the functioning of their offices and the importance of efficiency. It concerns an excellent sales rep who, on being promoted to the job of field sales manager, walked into his new branch office and realized that he knew absolutely nothing about its operation. He soon discovered that his secretary, whom he had inherited, was top-notch. So he called her in and said: "Mary, I'm a salesman and you're an office secretary. I'm going to spend my time out in the field getting business. You run this office and let me alone." At the same time the president, trying to cut expenses, was studying the branch office setup of his company. He called in each field manager to find out what he could learn about branch office operations. Needless to say, our friend made a very poor showing because he knew little or nothing about the office under his jurisdiction.

The moral of the story is that managers must be familiar with branch office procedures. They should seek to improve office operations, keep costs down, and increase the effectiveness of office personnel so that they can spend more time in the field and accomplish more when they are in the office. Managers may delegate office responsibilities, but they cannot abandon them.

Where their superiors have given them responsibilities beyond those involved in developing manpower, field sales managers may require a somewhat more complex office organization. But for managers who are simply line sales executives developing sales representatives, the office can be quite simple: a correspondence file; a file of statistical material for each sales rep and for the district or region as a whole; copies of invoices; a file folder for each task assigned to the manager, one for each sales rep, and one for his immediate supervisor; the controls used to manage the job; a manual of operations; and various necessary supplies. The rule to be followed is to keep the branch office simple, easy to use, uncluttered, and efficient.

6

Effective Communications

One vital function of the field manager as a developer of salespeople is communications. As shown in Figure 6-1, managers wield influence through their communications *upward* all the way to the board of directors. Top management cannot function effectively without knowing what is happening in the marketplace. Field sales managers are the people who can best communicate this vital information to the top officers. They also have considerable influence over the entire marketing organization beginning with their own bosses and continuing all the way down to the customers. Communicating *downward* though their sales reps, they supply to them and their customers the vital information that is the very foundation of the entire marketing operation. Let's examine what sorts of data pass through this vital communications center, the field sales manager.

Downward Communications

Assume that the president of the company has sold the board of directors on the idea of building a very large plant to manufacture product line B. Finally, the plant is ready to start operations. The board turns to the president and, in effect, says: "You wanted this plant. Now that you have it, keep it operating at full production and make it pay." The president instructs the marketing vice president to get on the ball, and this directive seeps down. The job of selling the production of this plant is spread throughout the organization. Eventually, as field sales manager, you are told of the

Figure 6-1. The field sales manager's communications network.

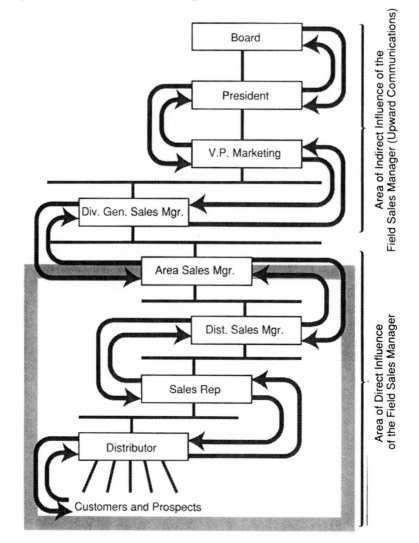

"piece of the pie" that you are required to take and that you in turn divide among your salespeople. Coming as it does from the very top, this message urgently requires the very best of communications. All sales reps are given to understand that, while they are expected to maintain their sales of product lines A, C, D, and E, they *must* reach their quotas on product line B. You are the one who must help them develop the skills that will enable them to do this. The real job of selling the output of the new mill is done by the sales reps, and you as the field sales manager assume the key responsibility for getting the job done.

Similarly, you must transmit and gain acceptance of the objectives that each sales rep must achieve during the current period and that concern the sales rep's personal development; you must communicate and gain acceptance for company policies and procedures; transmit valuable product or market information to the sales reps; and do all these things in a manner that will hold the sales reps' attention.

The most effective communication is accomplished on a face-to-face basis. Instruction, criticism, and coaching are most effective when performed by the manager in the field with the salesperson. The telephone is a valuable medium for exchanging data, but it is primarily informational and not recommended for instruction, much less criticism. Mail communications may be used to advantage in a number of ways. A letter can be used effectively to commend a sales rep, to confirm a personal conversation or phone call, to reduce to writing some specific directions, to prepare for some action to be taken, or to record an agreement. Printed matter sent to the sales rep usually consists of either important information to be preserved—technical data, price information, and important sales ideas—or informational data that need not be preserved—contest standings and a variety of other matters of passing interest. Important communications should be on a special form to be preserved, whether that be a manual page or a special technical data sheet, and marked in such a way that salespeople know where to file it in a special binder or file provided for that purpose. This ensures that valuable information is not mislaid or thrown away by sales reps. When printed matter is sent to salespeople, it is often helpful to attach a memo explaining the purpose of the material and how it can be employed most effectively.

In too many instances valuable bulletins and technical data sent to sales reps are never digested or, in some cases, even read. Salespeople are not students by nature, nor are they always great readers.

Long, wordy bulletins, stuffy manuals, and voluminous letters are often neglected simply because sales reps tend to be active people. When they get back to their office or home, they have little time or inclination to wade through such material. One helpful technique is to reduce material to the more easily readable form of charts or graphic outlines. Companies spend large amounts to make sure that their messages get through to customers and prospects. Perhaps it would pay them to spend some time finding out how to get through to the salespeople who represent them before these customers and prospects. Then when field sales managers communicate down to their sales reps, they will know that someone is listening.

Upward Communications

The people in top management must know how their products are being received, how well their policies are accepted, what their competition is doing, what is working well, where mistakes have been made, and what is being done to correct them. They must be advised of changing customer needs that will require new products or modifications of present products. Or perhaps new techniques devised by an ingenious sales rep are so effective that the entire organization should know about them. How is the company's advertising going over? These and scores of similar questions can best be answered by management's representative in the field—the field sales manager. If you are alert to this very important responsibility, you will allot specific time in the field for this very purpose. You may spend time with one of the best sales reps in your district just to observe and report on the sales techniques used. Or you may spend several days in the field to determine why sales to a certain class of trade or of particular product lines are moving too slowly or why they are greater than normal. This is the sort of information you will want to pass along up the chain of command.

Some field sales managers feel that their superiors do not heed their reports. If this is true and if the fault lies with a supervisor who lacks understanding of his or her place in the organization, this is indeed unfortunate. There may be little a manager can do but live with it until those higher up rectify the situation. More often the reason why managers are not being heard is that their method of communication is poor. For instance, as manager, you may transmit your views or findings in a form difficult to grasp, or one that shows inadequate preparation. If your reports are presented with

Figure 6-2. Sample form for a suggested change in policy.

Date: _____   From: _____

Present Policy:

Advantages	Disadvantages

Suggested New Policy:

Advantages	Disadvantages

Summary:

_____

rancor or in anger, their effectiveness is diluted. You must realize that your supervisors are just as busy as you are and often just as frustrated by their many responsibilities. They want to have material submitted to them in a concise, clear form so that they can make a prompt decision. It is preferable therefore that material submitted to superiors for a decision be in such form as only to require a yes or no. Figure 6-2 illustrates one suggested form for such reports.

Field sales managers should realize that it is not unnatural for the people above them to resent being told that they are wrong or do not know their business, especially by lower-level personnel. A softer approach is suggested. Rather than saying, "Such and such a policy is insane," and so on, you will do better to say: "I have some doubts as to the efficacy of such and such a policy and, having studied its effect on customers and salespeople, wish to suggest some changes, which are attached." You may submit several copies of your suggestions, stating that your purpose is to save the time of your supervisor should he wish to forward the idea upward for consideration by others.

One of your important functions as field sales manager is to report on your progress toward your assigned objectives, or lack of it, to your superiors. As a field sales manager you should expect the same kind of help from your immediate supervisors as you give to your salespeople. To receive it, you must keep your supervisor informed of (1) the objectives toward which each of your salespeople has agreed to work; and (2) the progress of each of your reps toward those objectives, together with the next steps you propose to take for the further development of each rep. For instance, where management has indicated deep concern about sales of product line B, it is not enough for you to tell your supervisor that your people are "on the ball" and working toward their assigned objectives with this product line. Management usually wants something more specific, the details of what each sales rep is accomplishing in this important area. Can the rep effectively present this product line? Is it being offered to all accounts that can use it in volume? How many accounts in each territory are potential purchasers of this product? How many have already bought it? At how many accounts is the product at least under serious consideration?

Where a sales rep is not effective in selling this product line, you can report to your supervisor what steps you are taking to correct the situation and perhaps request your supervisor's help in overcoming some obstacle. Good communications of this kind enable your supervisor to assist you with suggestions, new directions, or even help in the field. Regular reports keep your supervisor informed of your progress in attaining agreed-upon objectives and enable this key person to be helpful in your development. You should report to your supervisor with these ends in mind, thereby developing a sound two-way flow of communications that helps each of you to do a better job.

Despite the obvious advantages of an unrestricted flow of information, barriers to upward communications sometimes develop. These include, but of course are not limited to, the following:

1. To protect a likable manager, a sales rep may withhold bad news or uncomplimentary reports.
2. If the manager is "throwing his weight around," the salespeople may be afraid to press their dissatisfactions.
3. If the manager has failed to take action regarding undesirable conditions previously reported, the sales rep may feel that further reports would be useless.
4. When the manager doesn't listen or dismisses the subject, the sales rep may stop communicating.

If as a manager you are negligent about your salespeople's

communications, you may well be jolted by the sudden resignation of a good sales rep. You must listen when the sales rep is talking, and you must listen with an open mind and a willingness to consider suggested changes. In conclusion, let me emphasize that communication is an integral and important part of the entire management function. But it cannot be conducted in a vacuum; it must be considered as an aid in achieving the objectives set with each salesperson. The wise manager is as careful in communicating with each sales rep as in communicating with the company's most important account.

All this spells *teamwork*, which may well become the management buzzword of the 1990s—and it certainly has its place in field sales management. Under the guidance of a motivating sales manager, sales reps can put their heads together and run their area of operations to great effect. Teamwork inspires innovation. As an alert field sales manager, you should build such a relationship with your sales reps that ideas can flow freely from one to the other. Communications of this kind stimulate and maintain high morale and are of incalculable value to the entire organization.

Compensation for the Sales Force

Few first-echelon sales managers have anything to say about the compensation plan for their salespeople. This plan is usually developed at headquarters and handed down to field managers to administer. It is their function to explain and interpret the plan to their salespeople, making sure that they understand it and accept it as fair and sound, and to notify higher management of any general dissatisfaction with the plan. They may also suggest improvements in the plan or its administration. To do all this intelligently, field sales managers must understand certain basic principles about compensation administration.

It is clear that, out of every sales dollar, there must come money for raw materials, manufacturing, materials handling, office and selling expenses, taxes, and profits. There are only 100 cents in every sales dollar, and these pennies are divided in various ways. Management must decide how many of these pennies should go to the salesforce for marketing the product. Field sales managers do not decide this. But they do have an important voice in communicating downward to their people management's thinking with respect to the adequacy of the compensation. And they do have a responsibility to inform their superiors should they or their sales-people regard the compensation as inadequate for the job demanded.

The question of basic compensation has filled many pages with discussions of salary versus commission, size of salary, amount of drawing account, and the like. What the field manager must understand is that the company must receive profitable sales for the money it pays out to the sales reps as their compensation. The fact that a rep's sales volume may fluctuate widely from week to week and month to month, the likelihood that new salespeople or reps assigned to new territories will develop sales more slowly than those better established, together with other considerations, have led to an established policy of regularly paying some fixed amount of money to the sales force. Companies realize that salespeople's personal expenses never cease. They must pay rent, buy food and clothing, pay doctor bills, and so on. If they are tense because of fears that they will be unable to meet their current obligations, they obviously cannot perform at their best. What is worse, they cannot learn and improve themselves; they do not possess learning readiness because of their concern over paying their bills. In short, the field sales manager cannot do an effective job with sales reps who are worried about their finances. Consequently, their basic compensation benefits the company as well as the individuals receiving it. It should be large enough to cover the basic requirements of sales reps and to permit them to live on the level to which they have been accustomed. Some companies emphasize this primary purpose of the salary or drawing account by varying the amount that different sales reps may draw in accordance with their actual needs. Thus a single salesperson, who may require less money than one who is married, would receive a smaller salary. The married rep with children would receive the largest salary. Thus the salary or drawing account is not a measure of the sales rep's worth but simply a device to provide him or her with some regular income to meet current financial needs. Added to this basic compensation is an incentive or additional compensation that more truly reflects the sales rep's worth to the company and that more appropriately rewards individual achievement. Almost all sales compensation plans have built-in incentive features, either on the basis of individual or group performance. Incentive payments in some form are essential and fundamental to sales management.

A monetary incentive is, nevertheless, no substitute for good sales management. It cannot make up for poor selection, training, or supervision of sales reps. The job of the field sales manager is to improve the performance of the salespeople under him. Part of this function, as we know from the cycle of management, is to set objectives for growth and development and then to measure performance against these agreed-upon objectives. Certainly, there must be a determination of whether the sales rep is giving the company its money's worth. On the one hand, the manager must know whether a sales rep is happy with the compensation; but he must also be sure that the company is getting a proper return from that salesperson. Compensation is an incentive only in its broadest sense. There is reason to question its value as an incentive for accomplishing particular tasks in an above-average manner. Compensation should include incentives for above-average performance of the entire job. Management achieves motivation not only with money incentives but in the manner described in Chapter 4 under that heading.

Finally, it is important that managers be fully aware of the fringe benefits given to sales reps under the compensation plan. These may be very substantial. Because they are often overlooked by salespeople in appraising their compensation, managers should help their sales reps to understand and appreciate their value.

Well-paid salespeople make for a vital, satisfied sales force. Compensation that helps sales reps achieve a higher standard of living while at the same time lowering company selling costs is the most satisfactory. Good sales reps like compensation plans that place no ceiling on their earnings. They appreciate incentives that stimulate them to good total performance. It has been well said that the vital question is not how much money salespeople receive but how much money they earn.

7

District Sales Meetings

Almost every field sales manager who supervises five or more people is expected to hold district sales meetings periodically. There are, of course, some exceptions—for example, the manager whose sales reps are so widely scattered that it would be impractical to bring them together for a meeting. Normally this is not the situation. There are meetings of many types and for a wide variety of purposes. Let's consider some of them.

To begin with, there is the meeting where the sales reps are in reality only an audience. The speakers may include a top executive who comes from headquarters to report on "the state of the union" and to exhort the troops to greater efforts; the field sales manager who can always find plenty to talk about; a technical staff member from production, engineering, or research to introduce a new product or new uses for old ones; or perhaps a market research analyst to talk about the latest findings. The danger in this kind of meeting is that the sales reps may lose interest because they do not feel sufficiently involved. Salespeople are not accustomed to listening to others for long periods. Their attention is easily lost. A little of this kind of presentation goes a long way, and the better district meetings do not include more than one hour a day of such oratory.

The meeting may be one that is planned around such activities as role playing, films or slides, and management games to provide experience in decision making, in improving communications, or in solving problems. These are training exercises in skill building and habit development. Many people have used these techniques with considerable success. Handled by skilled professionals, devices such as role playing have produced good results. There is some question, however, as to the ability of most field sales managers to prepare and conduct effective role-playing sessions or in-basket exercises. When not conducted in a professional manner, these exercises are a waste of time and embarrass the participants. Although sometimes amusing, they are rarely productive of anything the sales reps can use to improve their effectiveness.

The field sales manager is faced with the necessity of planning a meeting that keeps the reps on their toes, stimulates and interests them from beginning to end, and helps them crystallize ideas that they can put to practical use. There is a limited amount of time, usually one day but sometimes only a few hours, so it is necessary to make the most of every moment. Recognizing this, I will describe a type of district sales meeting that every field sales manager can plan and conduct effectively, and that will send the salespeople home feeling that their time has been well spent because they have obtained some valuable ideas that can be put to practical use at once.

The meeting should be planned by the field sales manager with the help of his salesforce. It calls for full participation by every sales rep in attendance. It is essentially an exchange of experiences—all related to a specific subject under discussion—that enables the salespeople to learn from one another. Views are exchanged on such subjects as how to overcome specific customer objections, how to close orders of various types, how to meet servicing problems, how to plan effectively, and how to use sales tools in new ways. Such a meeting can also be used to introduce a new seasonal campaign or a new product and to resolve some of the problems relating to its introduction. It can make recalcitrant sales reps want to learn from their manager after they hear how helpful others have found such instruction. It can motivate them to accept and try the methods their manager has been suggesting to them. Nevertheless, it must always be remembered that this kind of meeting cannot do the job the field sales manager must do in the field with each of his people. It supplements the manager's field work but can never replace it.

Planning the Meeting

First of all, there must be a good reason for the meeting, one that is important enough to the sales reps to make them want to come and participate. It must also be important to you as manager and to the company. You should never call a meeting just for the sake of getting the gang together.

There are many important reasons for holding a district sales meeting. At the beginning of a new season, you may want to organize one around the best methods for successful sales planning and operations, featuring special techniques for getting customers to order early and purchase their full requirements, for determining the needs of customers, for making customers aware of their needs, and for emphasizing special selling points related to specific seasonal products. No matter what the occasion for the meeting, you should apply the following checklist:

1. Be clear about your reason for holding the meeting.
2. Establish the subject matter of the meeting.
3. Estimate the cost of the meeting.
4. Obtain authority, if necessary.
5. Determine who will attend.
6. Make a firm reservation for space.
7. Arrange for meals and other details.
8. Select and notify those who will prepare presentations.
9. Send out notices giving the time, place, and purpose of the meeting together with information as to how long it will last, what preparation is desirable, what should be brought to the meeting, the suggested method of travel, and the policy on reimbursement for expenses.
10. Prepare a precise agenda, including the subjects to be covered and the amount of time to be allotted to each subject.
11. Write out the kinds of questions you will put to the reps to keep the discussion going. Find individuals you can use to answer certain questions that may arise.
12. Determine how the meeting room is to be set up and advise those in charge to have the room so arranged—for example, with a round table, random seating, or V-shaped arrangement. Figure out where you will sit. Arrange for any displays. See that blackboard, chalk, eraser, water, glasses, and ashtrays are provided and properly placed.
13. Review the entire plan several times.
14. Inspect the physical facilities before the meeting takes place to make sure that your instructions have been carried out.

A good sales meeting should be an exchange of information and experience by those in attendance. As chairperson, you may

Figure 7-1. Variant discussion patterns at a sales meeting.

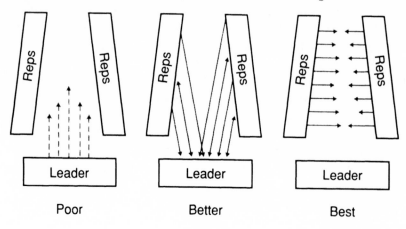

guide and stimulate the proceedings, but essentially your function is to keep the meeting lively, on schedule, and perhaps most important of all, on the subject under discussion. At the conclusion of the meeting, you will normally summarize the proceedings. Figure 7-1 illustrates three different ways in which the discussion can flow at sales meetings. Discussion among the reps themselves is obviously the most useful.

Sales meetings may also be held to emphasize the importance of a specific product or product line, or to deal with certain dissatisfactions that are infecting the organization. There is no better way to handle gripes than to put them before a meeting and permit full and free discussion. This causes reps to withdraw complaints that are unjustified because they know that their peers will reject or ridicule them. As manager, you will quickly discover how general and serious the dissatisfaction really is. The discussion may also provide some answers to the problem. At all events, it will indicate to the salespeople that the company is not afraid to bring dissatisfactions out into the open. This strengthens morale and encourages reps to develop fresh ideas and methods for tackling the selling job. It gives the people in a district a feeling of belonging and being part of a group with common problems that must be faced and solved. A sales rep might say that what the company tells her to do may be fine for the North but just won't work in the South. But when other sales reps covering the same territories tell her that the company's ideas work fine in the South, she is likely to change her views and try to apply these ideas.

Having decided upon a reason for the meeting, you must develop a plan. What form should the meeting take? Should any headquarters people be involved? Should you prepare a presentation that will dominate the meeting? Should this meeting take the form of a classroom or a conference? How much time should be allotted to each part of the meeting? Should only the older reps be asked to attend or should you mix veterans with newly developed sales reps? Let's consider some of these questions.

To begin with, you must decide what subjects you want to cover and determine their relative importance. If the meeting is to be for one day, you know the approximate number of hours available. You may decide to allow an hour for airing complaints and to devote the balance of the morning to product line B. After an hour for lunch, you may spend the entire afternoon exploring new ideas on effective planning of interviews and means of overcoming certain serious obstacles that are cutting into sales. This is, of course, only an example. The point is that you must list the subjects you wish to cover and determine their relative importance and position in the program. It is unwise to schedule a very important subject for late in the meeting when the reps are getting tired and beginning to look at their watches. It should be covered while they are fresh, alert, and most interested.

Having done this, you can decide whether any of your people can make a special contribution to the meeting by talking about some techniques they have used successfully, how they overcame certain types of sales resistance, novel uses for products they can share, or their outstanding selling performances. Reps selected for such a contribution should be notified in advance and told what is expected of them so that they can prepare. They should be invited to contribute in such manner that they will feel honored to have been selected. They must be told how long they will have the floor, and their method of presentation should be discussed in advance. An informal talk is always preferable to the reading of a written speech. Such a talk should consume no more than three to five minutes. If one of the reps has slides to show, this can be helpful to the audience and will add to the interest of the presentation. Renting or borrowing a projector and screen should present absolutely no problem.

Regarding who should attend, experience suggests the desirability of inviting all sales reps in the district or region regardless of their length of service. The older reps can contribute much and perhaps learn some new tricks. They can be given a feeling of importance or perhaps some recognition. The new sales reps will benefit from the experience of the older people and at the same time may impart some of their drive and enthusiasm to the veterans.

It is generally desirable that no person above the level of field sales manager be permitted to attend. Informality and freedom of expression are what you should aim for, and a room lined with "big brass" can easily cast a pall over the meeting. When the brass end up doing most of the talking, you, the field sales manager, are in danger of losing control of it. At times it may be desirable to have a product manager or a marketing, laboratory, or engineering person present at the meeting to make a technical presentation of predetermined length and at a specified time. This kind of a contribution, however, should never dominate the meeting or consume more than 25 percent of its time. The meeting should be conducted mostly by the sales reps themselves. Acting as chairman, your functions are (1) to keep the meeting on the beam and not let it wander from the subject at hand; (2) to make sure that every rep participates, encouraging those who are hesitant to speak; (3) to control the inevitable loquacious ones who would otherwise hog the meeting; (4) to summarize what has come out of each segment of the program so that each rep clearly understands the valuable parts; and (5) to pull together the entire subject matter at the end of the meeting, pointing up what the salespeople can put to immediate use in the field.

To get the meeting off to a good start, you may begin by saying:

> Our first topic today is product line B. Mike, you have done a top job with this line.

You may then proceed:

> Jill, have you anything to add to what Mike has said or do you have a different approach?

If you are asked a question, such as how you would meet some problem in selling this line, you should simply bounce it back to the group by asking: "Sam, what do you have to say about that?" In effect, as chairman, you are involving the reps in a discussion of their common problems, from which certain conclusions will be reached:

Bill, have you gotten anything of value from this discussion?
Let me summarize what seem to be the salient points of our
discussion.

When the time allotted for any matter has been used up, you will
say:

Well, we have discussed this long enough and I'd like to go on
to the next item on today's agenda.

This sort of meeting, because of the intense involvement of each
person attending, accomplishes a great deal in a single day. It "gets
across quick." Where a district is very compact, the reps can meet
at 10 A.M. and adjourn at 3 or 4 P.M., thus giving them time to
make a round-trip drive all in one day. In such cases the meeting
usually continues right through the lunch hour, with box lunches
served at the conference table. Where the salespeople must travel
greater distances, the meeting may be scheduled for a full day, with
reps arriving the night before and leaving the next night at the
adjournment of the meeting. Of course there may be instances where
a full district meeting is not feasible because of distances, costs, and
the amount of time that would be lost from work. In general, it is
best to hold the meeting in a hotel or motel where there will be no
interruption. It is important to detail the estimated cost before the
meeting. Such a meeting need not be costly. It is not intended for
the entertainment of the reps but is strictly a business meeting. If it
is not overly long, you can reduce to a minimum the time the reps
are away from the field.

To summarize, the most effective district or regional meeting
is one where you make the reps feel that it is *their* meeting. Your job
is to keep the salespeople involved at all times, to see that the discussion does not go astray, and to make sure that conclusions are
drawn that will help the reps when they return to their territories.
No agreement should be forced on the reps. *It is the discussion that is
important, not whether agreement is reached.* If one person talks too much,
you must say something like this:

Bill, you have made a wonderful contribution today, but let's
give some of the others a chance to express themselves.

If a new rep fails to participate, you may say:

Janet, we haven't heard from you on this subject. What do you think about it?

If several people are talking at once, you must bring the meeting to order and tell them that each person will get a turn to be heard. If two people are whispering to each other, it is usually sufficient to ask them to give the meeting the benefit of their discussion. A blackboard is handy for making important points and summarizations, and reps who wish to use the board should be encouraged to do so.

I recommend using a light, airy meeting room that is equipped with comfortable chairs, pads and pencils, a blackboard with chalk and eraser, and perhaps a slide projector and screen. A break of five or ten minutes every hour and a half will keep the group from growing restless.

8

Recruiting, Selecting, and Training New Sales Reps

For many field sales managers, recruitment occupies a considerable amount of time, keeping them from the other important tasks I have been discussing. (Not all field sales managers have this responsibility. Nevertheless, they often have to interview new sales reps before they are assigned and, because they are responsible for sales results in their districts, have the right to accept or reject the candidate.) Finding sources of eligible people, maintaining contact with them, and interviewing applicants is time-consuming. When this task becomes urgent because of an unstaffed territory, you may be pressed to drop everything else and devote yourself exclusively to the task of finding a sales rep to fill the vacancy. You cannot dodge this responsibility. You may put off recruiting by pleading the priority of other duties, but sooner or later it will catch up with you, and you will then be under tremendous pressure to fill one or more gaps in your district or region without delay.

How can you discharge this obligation without doing it under pressure and without slighting your other responsibilities? And another factor must also be considered. Because new sales reps are selected from those who have been recruited, the quality of the sales force under you will depend largely on the development potential of the people you recruit. Those recruited under pressure are not as likely to measure up to the necessary standards as are those recruited in a deliberate and planned manner. If you are not careful in this regard, you may find yourself saddled with a mediocre sales rep on whom you spend an inordinate amount of time trying to make "a silk purse out of a sow's ear." You will inevitably fail and then have the whole job to do over again. In the meantime your own performance in the entire district will have suffered.

What I am trying to emphasize is that the recruitment function is extremely important, not only to the field sales manager but to the company as well. The problem is to find methods whereby this job can be done thoroughly and well, yet without too great an expenditure of time. All companies have developed their own policies governing the recruitment and selection of salespeople and most expect their field sales managers to do the recruiting. Some companies have field recruiters who contact universities, employment agencies, and other sources; but even in these companies the field sales manager also is required to find good new sales material. Although many companies require a recruit to be interviewed at headquarters, where the final selection is made and the person is actually hired, still in the majority of cases the final selection will not be made unless the field sales manager approves it. So while there are instances where the field sales manager has nothing to do with recruitment or selection, this is unusual. Because the final selection is "your baby" to train and develop, you should be vitally interested in those recruited.

The average field sales manager requires only about two to four new reps a year. This is a very important statistic. Field sales managers who rationalize their failure to turn up suitable recruits by saying that good people are almost impossible to find or that college graduates "don't go for selling as a career," ignore the fact that they need find only three or four recruits in an entire year. Whatever the difficulties, any good recruitment program should be able to turn up that number without any trouble. It is not uncommon for a company to interview several hundred people initially and to eliminate by stages all but the three or four who will finally be employed. Because the number to be employed is low, the standards can be kept high. Although standards should never be lowered, it is understandable why they may inadvertently slip when large numbers of salespeople are being employed. But when only three or four are to be selected during an entire year, the field sales manager can be very selective and adhere rigidly to the established standards.

Just what is meant by standards? Either the company or the field sales manager must set some kind of standards. When you understand your stake in the person to be employed in terms of work load, training time, and field work at the sacrifice of other tasks, you will require standards for the person to be recruited regardless of whether your company has them. These standards, also called specifications, must be of two kinds. First, as field sales manager, you must have in writing what can be called *job specifications.* This is a list of all the things that the sales rep will be expected to do, with emphasis on the more important tasks. Figure 8-1 is such a list. Secondly, looking at this list, you might well ask yourself: "What kind of people must I find to perform all these tasks, what qualities must they possess, what sort of background?" If you were to write down your answers to these questions, they would be your *staffing specifications.* These are the two important tools you need before you can start recruiting. The people you want must have all or most of the qualities listed in the staffing specifications.

In key account selling, however, the specifications would be somewhat different because here it is mandatory for the salesperson to know quite a bit about the customer's business. At this level of selling, the salesperson develops a relationship with a customer that could be described as a partnership, acting as an adviser and diagnostician to the customer. The sales rep is also an educator, and brings to the customer the newest ideas, technological findings, and skills relevant to that business. In this case, a high degree of knowledge and experience in a particular business, enabling the rep to diagnose, advise, inform, and educate a customer, would be more valuable than any past sales experience.

Another tool the field sales manager must have for recruiting purposes is some document or brochure describing the company—its history, the kinds of products it makes, the markets it serves—as well as the job its salespeople are expected to do. In addition, this literature should outline the growth opportunities afforded sales reps within the company. Many companies prepare elaborate booklets for recruiting purposes. Whether or not the company furnishes such material, you as field sales manager should have something of this type. It may be just three or four mimeographed pages stapled together and headed "The Jones Manufacturing Company and Its Opportunities" or "A Future With Jones." If you prepare it yourself, you should send it "upstairs" for higher-level approval first.

(text continues on page 137)

Figure 8–1. A listing for job specifications for sales reps.

Principal Responsibilities	*How Measured*
Market Analysis	■ % of accounts identified ■ Potential of accounts identified ■ % of sales to potential

Sales Volume:
    Existing Accounts
    New Accounts
	■ % of $ quota attained
	■ Number of units sold
	■ Gross sales by product
	■ Product mix/market mix
	■ Profitability
	■ Target accounts penetration %
	■ Number of orders
	■ Average order value
	■ Call to order ratio
	■ Demonstration to order ratio

New Account Development	■ New accounts identified vs. other territories ■ New accounts penetrated and extent of penetration ■ Number of calls made vs. new accounts attained
Key Account Management	■ Number of key accounts ■ % $ penetration vs. $ potential ■ Cooperation for growth ■ Problems/opportunities identified and plans implemented ■ $ sales
Account Penetration	■ Accurate standard analysis method for all accounts ■ % $ penetration vs. $ potential ■ % vs. other territories vs. all territories
Territory Plans and Forecasts	■ % of forecast $ vs. $ of total potential ■ % of forecast vs. $ of total potential against territories ■ Days, weeks, months planned in advance

Figure 8-1. (cont.)

Principal Responsibilities	How Measured
Territory Plans and Forecasts (continued)	▪ Miles driven per $ in new sales vs. other territories ▪ Phone appointments made ▪ Analysis of quarter's activities vs. plan ▪ Territory expense as a % of sales ▪ Zones established ▪ Routes followed
New Product/Program Introductions	▪ Sales $ of new products/promos vs. other territories ▪ % of total account penetration per new product/program introduced ▪ Product mix vs. national figures ▪ Dealer stocking $ ▪ Dealer promotions implemented ▪ Dealer meetings
Sales Call Preparation and Analysis	▪ Prospects/customers uncovered and identified and recorded in account files, book (data base) ▪ Account objectives, plans set and implemented ▪ $ value per call ▪ Product mix/call ▪ Products per order ▪ Order/call ratio ▪ Units per order ▪ Average order value ▪ Demos per call ▪ Presentations planned (precall planning sheet) ▪ Call objectives reached ▪ Postcall analysis made ▪ Briefcase organization ▪ Trunk and home organization

(continues)

Figure 8–1. (cont.)

Principal Responsibilities	How Measured
Dealer/Distributor Development	<ul><li>Sales per distributor</li><li>Average sales per distributor vs. national figures</li><li>Average dealer growth over past five years vs. national figures</li><li>Dealer/distributor business plans in operation.</li><li>Distributor/dealer reviews per year at owner management level</li><li>Training/promotion meeting workshops conducted</li><li>Dealer/distributor reps worked with (time and orders)</li></ul>
Administration/ Communication	<ul><li>Quality time and number of personal vs. telephone contacts with area sales manager, branch administration</li><li>Reports in on time</li><li>Quality of reports</li><li>Number/quality of special reports</li><li>Errors per order written and delivered</li><li>Car neatness and organization</li></ul>
Expense Management	<ul><li>Expense vs. sales</li><li>Expense reports in on time and accurate</li></ul>
Competitive Products	<ul><li>File established and kept up to date as to prices and model changes</li><li>Knowledge of background and habits of competitive reps</li></ul>
Attitude Maintenance	<ul><li>Quality of attitude, judged by area sales manager, branch staff, key distributors and accounts</li></ul>

Figure 8–1. (cont.)

Principal Responsibilities	How Measured
New Sales Rep Training	▪ Number trained ▪ Quality of training as judged by training evaluations
Innovative Contributions	▪ Innovative/creative reports and ideas submitted
Recruiting	▪ Number and quality of reps brought in for interview and hired
Self-Development/Career Planning	▪ Written plan to area manager ▪ Grades and number of courses attended ▪ Items on career plan completed and improvements noted

Reprinted with permission from the 3M Corporation, St. Paul, Minnesota.

Sources of Recruits

Where does one find recruits? It's not hard for recruiters working out of headquarters to answer this question. Recruiting is their full-time job, and they can exhaust all known sources. But as field sales manager you just don't have the time to cover every possible source. You must understand that you cannot possibly do the job on a "crisis" basis. Recruitment must have continuity so that at all times you have a pool or reservoir of applicants, one or more of whom will be available when you need a new sales rep in your district or region.

How can you set up a continuous recruitment program that will not consume too much of your time and yet will produce the desired number of qualified new people? First, you limit the job and pare it down to a size you can supervise and control. You yourself must be a recruiter twenty-four hours a day and 365 days of the year, including Sundays and holidays. Wherever you go, you must keep an eye peeled for good sales material—in the office, on planes or trains, at church, at the club, on the golf course. Wherever you are, you must be continually on the lookout for sales talent and for ways of bringing it into the service of the company. You must be selling your company and its opportunities at all times. You cannot expect to turn up good prospects every day or every week. Keeping in mind that you will need only three or four new people each year, you will be patient but ever alert in your search for them. You are in fact your own best source of good material for the sales force.

Second, you should enlist the help of those salespeople whose judgment you respect and whom you feel are capable of spotting good sales material. These individuals should be used to bird-dog good prospective sales reps, flush them out, and then arrange for you to interview interested applicants. After all, who knows the job better than the sales reps themselves? If they are successful and enthusiastic about the job and company, they can impart this feeling to applicants. They can answer questions about the job and what it involves. They can even take applicants home and let them see how well successful company sales reps live. Sales reps also get into areas that recruiters rarely reach. In covering their assigned territory, they probably visit outlying sections for some of their calls. Some of the very best salespeople may be found buried in rural areas awaiting an opportunity that often never comes. Consider the young man in a small town who goes to work in a local factory, gets married and settles down. He cannot get out of his rut because he must work every weekday and does not want his boss to learn that he is looking for another job. On weekends when he is free, the interviewers in the big cities are not working. And so he remains where he is, awaiting an opportunity that may come only through a chance meeting with some sales rep. The job offered to him may be a once-in-a-lifetime opportunity, and he will make every effort to succeed in it. If the company is recruiting only people with technical backgrounds, this procedure may be much more difficult. Many companies have so thorough a training program that they can recruit people with little or no sales experience provided they have the basic qualifications. Sales reps may turn up excellent potential sales people among factory workers or reps employed in fields other than selling. The use of sales reps to comb the rural or small communities for good sales material constitutes an important part of any program of continuous recruiting.

Some companies compensate their sales reps for recruiting people. This is normally a policy matter determined at a level above the field sales manager. In any event, recruitment efforts are a valuable experience for sales reps, and you should point this out to those you select for this extra work. Here is a way for sales reps to learn some of the skills that prepare them for advancement—how to handle a responsibility beyond their primary responsibilities, and how to find and interview good sales material. You can encourage this activity by discussing each applicant with the sales rep who referred him and by using the experience to show the rep how to appraise and select salespeople. The point is that, even without monetary compensation to the sales rep for this help, the experience may be of such value as to make it interesting and worthwhile.

In building a continuous program of recruitment, the field sales manager can turn to a third excellent source of sales material—the *small* college. Within the district of almost every field sales manager, there are probably a number of small colleges. These schools are not inundated by recruiters coming to interview their graduating classes. They do not have highly sophisticated placement offices. But they often do have men and women with the best possible backgrounds for sales careers. I suggest that you establish a close relationship with just two such schools in your area. By this I mean that you should contact the placement officer, the deans, and perhaps the heads of the departments of economics, engineering, or business. Your purpose is to *sell* these people on the idea that your company is the best in its field, that it offers great opportunities, and that the school could do no better than to refer its top students to the field sales manager for an interview. This "hard sell" should lead the school's placement people to refer every promising graduate with the proper qualifications to you for an interview. The school's placement officials will also be alerted to refer to you any alumni who returned to the school for assistance in securing better employment. You should leave with the school authorities some copies of the company's application blank and some of the brochures that describe the company and the opportunities it offers. You might also ask the local sales rep, if qualified, to drop in occasionally to maintain contact with the school people and to keep the name of the company before them. This person should offer to talk with all applicants and answer any questions they might have before formally applying to you. This sort of contact with two small colleges should produce at least one good salesperson a year.

Another recruiting source is the employment agency. There has been much unfavorable comment on agencies as a source of manpower. Those who have had good results attribute this to their special relationship with the agency. I suggest that you select just two reputable agencies within your area and in each case speak to the head of the agency first. Adopting the same methods as those used for the interview with small colleges, you should sell the employment agency head on the wonderful opportunities offered by your company to people of high caliber who can meet its requirements. You should then speak to other agency personnel and sell them too. It is important not only to review carefully the qualifications for the job with agency personnel but also to supply them with application forms, company brochures, and the staffing specifications for the job.

This relationship should be renewed whenever you are in town, if only by a noon luncheon meeting with the agency personnel. If an agency habitually sends poor material, you should change agencies, always limiting yourself to two good agencies at any one time.

You have now developed a plan for continuous recruitment that is designed to produce up to five new salespeople a year. Hopefully you will not require that many, but in any case you have a pool of people who have been interviewed, have indicated an interest in working for the company, and who, even though presently employed elsewhere, will probably be available when a job opportunity opens.

If you can develop a pool of from five to ten such people, you will usually be on safe ground. When an opening occurs, you may find that your first and second choices in the pool are not available but that your third choice is also a sound selection. There is, of course, no guarantee that every individual in the pool will be available when wanted, but it is almost certain that at least one qualified person will be found. Handled this way, recruitment will no longer be on a "putting out a fire" basis but will be so designed as to fit in with your work load and time schedule.

Selecting Sales Reps

Selection begins with an interview. As field sales manager you will probably find these selection interviews highly disruptive of your schedule because they are time-consuming. However, there is a method that will conserve your time without diminishing the quality of the interview.

The first interview with the applicant is usually referred to as a screening interview. Its purpose is to eliminate applicants you do not wish to consider further and to lay a foundation for subsequent interviews with those in whom you are interested. How should this first interview be planned and executed? A good interview is a two-way affair. You want to learn the extent to which the applicant's qualifications meet the staffing specifications for the job. The applicant wishes to learn how well the job meets his or her requirements for security, opportunity for growth, valuable work experience, and job satisfaction. Both parties are interviewing; therefore, it should not be a one-sided affair. Nevertheless, as manager you should be in command of the interview, guiding and directing it from the very start.

Some preparation is expected of both individuals. You will have before you an application form giving information about the applicant. The applicant should have studied in advance the material describing the history of the company, the kind of business it conducts, the products it makes, the people to whom it sells, the duties and training of its salespeople, and their opportunities for advancement. I suggest, therefore, that when you receive the application form from a promising applicant you respond by setting an appointment for an interview at least ten days in advance and enclose a copy of the company's brochure. This appointment may be at your office or at a hotel in the town where the applicant resides. You can conserve time by making the appointment for late afternoon after your other work is concluded. If you are on the road, you can make the appointment for an evening so that it will not interfere with your other duties.

Although each manager will conduct the interview in his own way, there are certain guidelines that must be followed if the interview is to be of value. It is desirable to let the applicant do most of the talking. You need not be in a hurry to tell your story. The right kind of applicant will find out about the company by asking questions. The important thing is to listen attentively to what the applicant has to say. The applicant must be put at ease at the very start of the interview. You should greet him or her cordially, offer a chair (some interviewers come from behind their desk and sit casually beside the applicant), and place an ashtray nearby in case the applicant smokes. You should strike an informal note along these lines:

> Let's make this interview very informal. Please feel that this is *your* interview as much as mine. Your future is involved in whatever decision you make about this job. You might start by telling me what your long- and short-term goals are. Tell me anything about yourself and your history you feel I should know. Feel free to ask me any questions that come to mind about our company, its operations, and the job you are applying for. If this is satisfactory to you, suppose you start by telling me your reasons for applying for this job.

Now you must sit back and listen. What are you listening for? What are the things that should influence your decision on the applicant? Let's consider a few. A good sales rep is down-to-earth, realistic, with common sense. Are the applicant's goals realistic? Do they indicate an understanding of the painfully slow climb up through an organization, the need to work hard to achieve recognition by supervisors? Do the applicant's short-range goals suggest that he will stay with the job, or would he tend to become dissatisfied? Do his long-range goals take into consideration his family, his general growth and improvement? Does he show a real interest in making money and getting the things that money will buy? Is he ambitious to rise above his present level? A good salesperson is thorough. Does the applicant describe himself thoroughly? A sales rep must thoroughly inform customers about his products. If a product has eight key selling points, the manager wants all eight brought to the customer's attention. The applicant's thoroughness and ability in selling himself to you tell much about his potential as a sales rep.

A good sales rep works hard physically. Is the applicant a hard worker and does he come from a family of hard workers? Good salespeople are more likely to come from such backgrounds. Did the applicant work as a boy, during summer vacations or while at school? Did he earn at least part of his expenses if he went to college? A good sales rep must be energetic and capable of hard physical work. A good sales rep is "money hungry." He likes to be on top and to be a winner. Is the applicant competitive? Good sales reps usually are. Does the applicant want to make money, to lead the procession? Did he try to be a leader when he was at school? Does he seek prestige, recognition? A good sales rep is articulate. He can communicate well. How will the applicant sound in front of a customer? He need not speak "the King's English," but it is important that he be articulate and persuasive, that his voice be pleasant and well modulated. A good sales rep loves to sell. Does the applicant really want to be a salesman or is he just applying for a job—any job? Most successful salespeople would not take any other than a selling job. You can sound out the applicant by asking him whether he would be interested in a fine inside job.

Finally, a good sales rep is a good planner. Is the applicant one? Has she prepared for this interview by making a list of questions to be answered? She has had ten days or more to think about this interview and to prepare for it. Did she do any planning during this time? Sharp, penetrating questions by the applicant are a favorable sign—for example, "Do you promote from within?" "How will I be trained to do my job?"'"How do you measure the expected growth rate of a rep starting out like myself?" On the other hand, if the questions mostly have to do with fringe benefits, the applicant is hardly worth interviewing further. When she is questioning you, she can be expected to ask many specific questions about the company and the job opening. If she has no such questions to ask, there is no point to your volunteering the information. Unless the applicant indicates genuine interest, you might just as well save the time required for an exposition of the company, its opportunities and policies.

If your reaction is unfavorable, you can easily terminate the interview whenever the applicant says that she has no further questions. You may either tell the applicant at this point that she does not get the job or you may say that you wish to consider the matter and that the applicant will hear from you later on. Thus the screening interview has been considerably shortened without in any way reducing its quality. An unsatisfactory applicant has been eliminated with a minimum loss of time. If, on the other hand, the interview has aroused your interest in the applicant, you should respond by giving a complete exposition of the company, its opportunities, and the job itself. At this point the interviewer actually sells the job to the applicant. Figure 8-2 lists some questions that can be used to draw out the details of the candidate's background and work experience.

When this has been done and the applicant is ready to accept the job, you then back away gently, making the applicant follow after you and fight for the job. This is accomplished by making a statement such as:

> You have a very good job right now where you can probably move ahead. You have a wife and two small children to support. Considering your present nice income and family responsibilities, I wonder whether it is wise for you to change jobs, especially when you would, in coming with us, be getting into an entirely new field, where you have no assurance of success and might conceivably find yourself out of a job and in a tight spot financially. You had better consider the seriousness of the move you are making and be sure you want to take the risks involved.

Now you are testing the aggressiveness of the applicant. You want a salesperson who will not easily take no from a customer and who

Figure 8-2. Questions calculated to reveal an applicant's motivation and background.

1. Why have you applied for *this* job?
2. What is there in your past experience that you want to tell me about, that you feel would add to your qualifications for this job?
3. What do you know about this company and its products and services?
4. You are about to change jobs. This involves some adjustment on your part. How do you see yourself coming into a new organization? What steps do you see as important? What possible obstacles or difficulties concern you?
5. Is there anything in your life-style that would make it unpleasant for you to travel frequently or even to be transferred to another territory?
6. As a salesperson, how would you be helpful to our customers?
7. What questions do you wish to ask me about this job?
8. Even though you know very little about this company, try to tell me how you see yourself working at this job on a typical day.
9. What did you like and dislike about your previous job, and why did you leave?
10. Did you earn money during your school years? How?

will fight back and try to get the order. Will the applicant now show this quality?

As has been demonstrated, a good interview can bring to the surface some of the intangible qualities so important to success in selling: thoroughness, ability to plan, drive or competitive spirit, aggressiveness, articulateness. Above all other qualities, a company must insist that the person who represents it have character. No company can afford to be represented by someone lacking in personal integrity.

Another important consideration that you must always keep in mind when interviewing is the cost of employing, training, and developing a new sales rep; nor must you forget the many hours required by preparing for and actually giving such instruction. Many companies spend in excess of $25,000 on a new sales rep during the first year, and as field sales manager you make great sacrifices in rearranging your work load and schedules to find the time to work with the new salespeople. While interviewing an applicant, you might well ask yourself: "Would I spend $25,000 of my own money on this person if I were in business for myself and he came to me for a job? Is he the kind of person I would be willing to eat my heart out for training and developing?''

Many companies use psychological tests of one kind or another. The use of such tests is a decision for higher management, and as field sales manager you usually have no say in the matter. You must follow company policy. Yet it is your responsibility to make the final decision on a job applicant. Test results may help you but are seldom a substitute for sound judgment. Tests can effectively screen out the least qualified, but they often cannot select the best people from among those who are acceptable. You must base your ultimate decision on what you have seen and heard in your interviews with the applicant, giving some weight to test results. In all cases this decision should be yours alone.

Before a final decision is made, the applicant's references must be thoroughly investigated. References should not be solicited by letter or printed form; a personal call should be made upon the applicant's previous employer. Where this is not feasible, a telephone interview may be substituted. Such an interview should be as carefully planned as an interview with an important account (see Figure 8-3). Most businesspeople hesitate to say anything that may keep a former employee from landing a good job. They want to be honest but at the same time they do not want to hurt the chances of the applicant. As interviewing manager you must therefore read between the lines, searching out the gray areas that you want to probe for more definite information. For instance, the previous employer may say that he considers the applicant to have been a good sales rep and to have performed very well under competent supervision. Further questioning, prepared in advance, may reveal that, while the applicant was a pretty fair salesperson, he wasn't good enough to measure up to *their* standards and that, although he did all right when someone was breathing down his neck, he did not perform as well without supervision. Thus the value of a reference depends, to a considerable degree, on how well the person checking the reference prepared for the interview.

Ordinarily, some two or three interviews are conducted before a person is employed. An applicant who looks very good at the first interview may seem less impressive on a subsequent one. Similarly, an applicant about whom you initially had some grave doubts may become your first choice after a second interview. Where the final choice is made at headquarters, it is very helpful if you send a thorough evaluation of the candidate to headquarters so that top man-

Figure 8-3. Sample letter and questions useful in checking references.

I'd appreciate your assistance in verifying some information and obtaining your comments and assessment of Mr./Mrs./Ms _____ who has applied to us for a position in _____. It costs us about $25,000 to employ and train a good person plus considerable time; therefore, we want to make sure that this is the right job for the applicant and that he or she is the right person for us. It would be most helpful if you could tell us a few things about the applicant. We will, of course, hold any information you share with us confidential. Any other comments you feel would be helpful to us or the applicant will be greatly appreciated. Thank you for your cooperation.

Take notes here:

Do you recall this person? (If not try and find the name of the person he worked for.)

The applicant is applying for a sales job in our organization. How do you think he/she would fit into that kind of work?

If he/she sold, was his/her volume and general performance in the upper third, the middle third, or lower third of your sales organization?

Was the applicant a hard worker?

How well did the applicant get along with his/her boss? With his/her fellow workers?

Did the applicant require a great deal of supervision or did he/she perform pretty much on his/her own?

Did the applicant accept supervision or was this a problem?

Did the applicant learn quickly and could he/she apply what was learned?

Would you rehire the applicant?

How well did the applicant perform the details of his/her job, paper work, and so on?

What were the applicants stronger points? Weaknesses?

Comments:

agement may have the benefit of your judgment. The second and third interviews are critical because this is when you willingly take the time to dig deeply into the applicant's work history, personal background, and general characteristics. No part of the applicant's past should escape thorough investigation, and the sales job should be explained to him or her in detail so that you have a clear picture of the person for whose services you are bargaining, and the applicant knows in detail the kind of job that is being offered.

Training New Sales Reps

Now that you have found and employed a promising salesperson, what are the methods you use to make sure that this new sales rep has every opportunity to succeed? In most companies there is a period of orientation and product training, which precedes the formal sales training conducted by the field sales manager. In some companies the newly employed sales rep is brought into headquarters for this orientation period. In other companies the new sales rep is trained wholly in the field and only brought into headquarters after having qualified for more costly and intensive training. It is almost universal, however, to assign the new rep to the field sales manager for *sales* training. In some cases this means that the newly employed sales rep travels with and works under a senior sales rep. This permits the new salesperson to observe the senior in action, to learn that the job can be done and just how it is done. With confidence bolstered by having observed another sales rep perform effectively, the new rep is ready to go out and try the job alone. In other cases the new sales rep is put directly to work and expected to produce sales at once.

There is a growing feeling in sales management circles that many good new salespeople are lost to the company because of inept handling during their first week or two in the field under the field sales manager. There is thought to be a widespread lack of understanding of new sales reps and the pressures under which they are working. To illustrate the problems facing the new sales rep, let's take as an example one who has received product training at headquarters and has been given some orientation as to the company and its policies, as well as some familiarity with the various forms used by salespeople such as order books, daily reports, expense reports, intracompany and intradepartmental correspondence. Let's further suppose that he is being relocated and that, although previously employed in St. Louis, he is to report to his field sales manager in Kansas City upon his return from headquarters training. His wife has taken care of having the furniture moved by van after flying down to Kansas City and locating an apartment. They plan to live in a motel until the furniture arrives. They have a baby, who is staying with the new sales rep's mother-in-law while all this is taking place. The couple are complete strangers to Kansas City. They have given their address to the company and find that there are several large cartons awaiting them at the empty apartment. These cartons were sent by the company and contain various samples to be used in selling, a large supply of literature covering some fifty different products, various special data sheets, policy and procedure manuals, order books, supply requisitions, expense reports, daily, weekly, and monthly reports and route sheets, and other stationery of various kinds. Add to this formidable array of material the fact that the new sales rep is under great tension to make good at his new job. He has given up a good position with another company and has moved to a strange city with his wife and baby. He wants very much to succeed. He feels lost being with a strange company in a new location. The van with his furniture has not arrived and his motel room is uncomfortably small. On top of this, his boss is busy and wants him to get going. His manager expects to start his formal training "next week" if he can find the time. In the situation just described, the new sales rep may easily be lost to the company. The vital learning readiness of the new salesperson is achieved partially through his own determination to learn and succeed but also as a result of his manager preparing him for the training experience in such a manner that his mind is not burdened with worries about his wife, his baby, his new apartment, his territory, his paperwork, his sales equipment, and so on.

When a new sales rep first arrives on the job, it is desirable that you make sure that learning readiness is present *before* he starts the training process. The following considerations are involved in such preparation for training. First, you should make sure that the new salesperson is comfortably settled in the new residence. If there is no relocation involved, this problem of course does not exist. On the other hand, in a situation like the example just given, you should instruct the new sales rep first to get his living arrangements straightened out and then to report for work. There is a corollary advantage in this course of action in that it will give you a preview of the new sales rep's ability to handle a problem quickly, decisively, and effectively. A resettlement that drags on for too long is not a good sign. Experience indicates that new salespeople should not require more than a few days to get settled domestically. They need not find perfect living quarters. They can use weekends to look for something more to their taste after they have lived in the new city long enough to learn a bit about the various locations and accommodations available. Once the new sales rep is settled domestically, I further suggest that you help him unpack all the equipment and material sent from headquarters and show him how to organize it for effective use. You will explain to the sales rep which of this material should remain in his home, which belongs in his car, how best to distribute it through the car, how to keep samples in good condition, and how to use the various forms properly.

Finally, you should show the sales rep how to cover the territory, acquaint him with its geography, and make sure that he knows how to identify a prospect so that he won't waste time on valueless calls. When the new sales rep's mind is at ease with regard to (1) domestic matters, (2) organization of tools, equipment, and office work, and (3) knowledge of the territory and how to work it, he is ready for instruction in sound sales techniques. It is now reasonably likely that he will absorb training, be able to apply the instruction, and make normal progress toward the goals that have been set for him.

There is quite a divergence of opinion concerning the relative effectiveness of learning by doing. To many people in management, it is inconceivable that much can be learned merely by observing another person in action. Let's take a very simple example—learning to drive an automobile. To an experienced driver, the automobile seems almost a part of him. He performs the necessary operations mechanically without consciously thinking about putting a key in the lock, releasing the emergency bake, setting the lever that puts the car in gear, turning the wheel, accelerating, or applying the brakes. Yet when this same driver tries to teach a teenager how to drive, he finds that the only way to do it properly is to place the teenager at the wheel and instruct him while sitting next to him, observing what he does wrong and correcting his mistakes. The student will never learn to drive the car simply by sitting next to the driver and observing him. Observation will never give him the feel of the car and the confidence that comes with experience.

It is generally accepted today that people learn best by doing and that teachers teach best by observing their students perform a function, correcting and encouraging them, and repeating the process until they can perform the task without any need for correction.

During World War II the government developed a teaching procedure called Job Instruction Training (JIT) that proved extremely effective in imparting skills to unskilled workers. The principles employed in this technique are entirely applicable to the training of salespeople. In essence this is how it works. First, place the trainee in front of the job she is to do and put her at ease. Then tell her exactly what the job is and have her repeat the description so that you know she understands what you have told her. Next, perform the task yourself exactly as you have explained it while she observes you. After the job is completed, review what you have done and have her tell you how to do the job and actually do it. Correct her when she makes a mistake, explaining her error and repeating the procedure as often as necessary. When she has completed the task, repeat the process until she is able to go through the entire operation without error.

How can this technique be applied to selling? When you are ready to teach sales techniques to the new sales rep, you both go to call on a prospect. On the way, you explain why this account is a prospect and why you have selected it for a call. The sales rep is put at ease while you explain exactly how you plan to make the call. You talk about each detail of the interview from the approach to the receptionist to the conclusion of the interview and the achievement of whatever objective was set for this call. As you talk, you arrange your equipment and sales tools for use in the interview. When you have completely planned the call, you ask the sales rep to review the steps briefly to determine how well your approach to planning has been absorbed. You and the sales rep then make the call together, but you conduct the entire interview; the sales rep acts only as an observer. After the interview you and the sales rep hold a curbstone conference to review all that happened during the interview, the extent to which the planning of the interview was followed, and the effectiveness of the planning. On the next call, you encourage the sales rep to do the planning out loud, correcting him until a fairly good finished plan is developed, and then tell him to make the call. The sales rep introduces you but without using your title. He then proceeds with the interview, paying no attention to you (who are now sitting a short distance away where you can follow the conversation without participating in it). The same technique of *entering and withdrawing*, described earlier as a training device for use with senior salespeople, may be employed with the new sales rep to "pick him up" should he stumble. In no case should you take the interview away from the new rep unless he "collapses" under tension or unless some other critical situation arises where, in your judgment, the welfare of the sales rep demands that you take control. Only the welfare of the new sales rep should be considered when you are deciding whether to take over. You must remember that more may be learned through failure than from success. It is often justifiable to let a rep fail and then point out his errors, show him how to overcome them, and let him try again and succeed through his own efforts.

While the new sales rep is getting started, you should keep in close touch with him. I suggest that first field contacts be at frequent intervals, but be spaced further apart as the sales rep progresses. For instance, after the first day, you might contact the sales rep again in three days. Or you might ask him to phone in every evening to report on what he has done each day, what problems he has run into, and what help he needs in overcoming sales resistance or other difficulties. The third contact may be a full week after the second, the fourth ten days later, the fifth after two or three weeks, until finally one field contact a month seems sufficient. If serious problems develop, it may become necessary to resume more frequent field contacts. During this entire period you are doing two things. First, you are trying to speed the growth, development, and productivity of this new salesperson; second, you are evaluating the sales rep to determine whether he continues to look as promising as he did at first. When a new salesperson is sincere, energetic, and honest, it is sometimes difficult to make a sound evaluation. Yet the company relies upon you to appraise his performance. The following procedure may help you in this connection.

At the conclusion of your first field contact, you and the sales rep reach agreement regarding the areas where the rep has shown strength and those where he must work harder to overcome apparent failings. This agreement on objectives for development is confirmed by your writing to the sales rep. At your next field contact, you carefully observe the degree to which the sales rep has tried to improve his performance. If he has ignored the areas of personal development that were agreed upon at the conclusion of the prior contact, you discuss this with him to find out why. If he has no good reason for failing to follow through on his training, you must again tell the sales rep what is expected of him; the same objectives must be set for your next field contact and again confirmed in writing. If on the next field contact there is still no evidence of any sincere effort by the sales rep to improve his performance in these same areas, you are obligated to explain to him that his success and his very continuance with the company depend on his ability to grow and develop. You explain that your role is one of teacher and helper to the sales rep, but that your effectiveness depends on the degree to which he applies himself to his own improvement. Thus the sales rep is warned that he had better make a real effort to master the training he is receiving. If by the next field contact you can still find no evidence of any real effort by the sales rep to follow your instructions, there is justification for discharging him. The deciding factor is the degree to which the sales rep is applying himself to the improvement of his weaknesses. The vital question is, *Is he really trying?* There is no purpose in butting your head against a stone wall by training a salesperson who isn't interested enough even to try to follow your guidance.

The second consideration is whether the salesperson has the ability to absorb and apply the training. Perhaps he is trying but is incapable of following instructions or of applying what he has been taught. Perhaps he isn't bright enough; perhaps he is emotionally disturbed by some personal matter. Whatever the reason, if the sales rep is not trying or appears incapable of learning and applying what he has learned, you and the company will be far better off without his services.

It has been said that new salespeople are like hurdlers in a race. They must jump a number of hurdles beginning with the first recruitment interview and continuing throughout their employment until they are fully integrated into the sales organization and given a senior's territory. Anywhere along the line they may fail to clear a hurdle and be separated. They can't win after they have knocked over a hurdle so it is pointless to let them keep running. It is the manager's responsibility to determine whether an important hurdle has been knocked over and then to act accordingly. Too often the manager is subject to wishful thinking about his salespeople. The rep about to be discharged may secure a lucky order, and the manager begins to hope that he may make good after all, in spite of his unfavorable performance rating. This is a mistake. You ought not to base a judgment on a single incident, good or bad. When the sales rep's overall performance indicates a course of action, then that action should be taken. Thousands of dollars have been lost by keeping poor salespeople on the payroll too long.

A Final Word

I have now come full circle in my discussion of the field sales manager's many areas of responsibility. Rather than summarize what has already been stated at length in the preceding chapters, it would be more helpful to conclude this book with a brief checklist that will help you to answer that all-important question: "Am I doing my job well?" You can be satisfied that you are performing your job as field sales manager well when:

1. You have a plan of action for yourself and for each of your salespeople.
2. You know that your plan is being carried out and that each of your reps *wants* to carry it out.
3. You know how well you are doing with regard to every task that has been assigned you.
4. You know the next step that you and each of your people must take to achieve your personal objectives.
5. You strive constantly to improve your own performance and that of your salespeople.
6. Your salespeople realize that they are doing a better job because of the help you have given them.

Index

LaVergne, TN USA
09 March 2010
175387LV00004B/77/A